The Team Lead Model Of Self Leadership

Application of Relational Leadership Concept to Self-Leadership and Effective Team Leadership

The Team Lead Model Of Self-Leadership

Application of Relational Leadership Concept
to Self-Leadership and Effective Team Leadership

FIRST EDITION

DR. JOE WOLEMONWU, DBA

All rights reserved.
Do Not reproduce, store in a retrieval system(s), or transmit, any part of this publication, in any form or by any means, electronic, mechanical, photocopying, recording, or otherwise, without the prior written consent of the author.

First Edition

Copyright © 2022, Dr. Joe Wolemonwu, DBA

REVIEWS

"This book is fascinating. It lays bare an inconvenient truth - every leader has a blind spot - and provides a framework to turn weaknesses into opportunities through self-leadership and team leadership. It is relevant in these trying times of a global pandemic as more demands are placed on public sector leaders. When I think about successful organizations that have navigated disruption, I can't find any without a good leader and a functional team. It reminds me of the Five Dysfunctions of a Team."

- Mr. Ernest Chrappah, MBA - Director, DC Department of Consumer and Regulatory Affairs (DCRA).

"This is a fascinating book on self-leadership! The topic of self-leadership has been at the forefront of university and college leadership courses for nearly three decades. Self-leadership allows a leader to influence others to act so that the goals of the organization are met. Leaders will ultimately succeed or fail based on their ability to effectively navigate their most important, complex, and relational situations. These are the difficult situations that leaders regularly encounter where there is no one right answer and successfully engaging others is critical for success. This book is a must-read for leaders who want to increase their self-awareness, emotional intelligence, inclusion, mindfulness, empathy, social intelligence, and learning agility."

- Dr. Corey Beckett - Lecturer, Public Administration University of Virginia, U.S.A.

TEAM LEAD

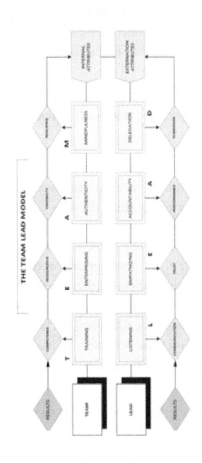

CONTENTS

Dedication ix
Acknowledgments x
Foreword xi
Preface xiii
Chapter 1: Introduction 15
Chapter 2: Origin of Self-Leadership 26
Chapter 3: Core Leadership Theory 34
Chapter 4: The Team Lead Model 41
Chapter 5: Relationship Between Constructs 68
Chapter 6: Self-Leadership Perception 88
Chapter 7: Self-Leadership Analysis 95
Chapter 8: Self-Leadership Traits 124
Chapter 9: Self-Leadership Strategy 130
Chapter 10: Application of Self-Leadership 138
Chapter 11: Relational Leadership 147
Chapter 12: Leadership Blindsports 152
Chapter 13: Leadership Reflections 160
Glossary 168
References 175
About The Author 218
Index 219
At A Glance 223

teamlead

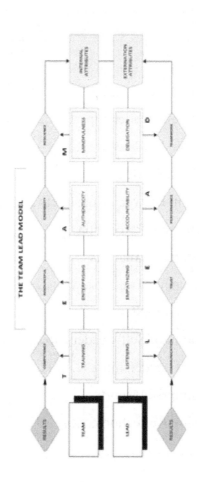

DEDICATION

I dedicate this book to my dad, Late Elder Boniface Nlerem Wolemonwu, who passed away on 02 February 2022, and whose contributions to my life molded me to be the leader and the man I am today. I remember the first lesson my father taught me as a young man: to always live a life of integrity. As a leader, I have come to the understanding that integrity builds trust, authenticity, and credibility, which eventually leads to a good reputation (which my dad calls "a good name"). In my entire life, one thing that remained constant is that my parents continually stood in the gap through their advice, encouragement, and prayers. I have lived by these moral principles as a leader. Dad, I know you are proud of the man and the leader I have become, I just wished you were alive to read this book, but I also know that you are smiling on the other side. Rest on, daddy!

ACKNOWLEDGMENTS

I would like to take this opportunity to thank the almighty God for making it possible for me to see the completion of this informative book. Also, I would like to thank everyone who supported me in getting this project done by reviewing the contents and making suggestions. During these last four years of research and writing this book, I learned that through determination, persistence, and the grace of God, you can accomplish whatever you set out to achieve.

A special thanks to my immediate family for their patience with me in the process of writing this book and even throughout my research to get this book done. This book would not have been complete without my family's support. To my mentors who reviewed this book and friends who motivated me to keep writing, I appreciate you all for the time you put into this book review, your encouraging words, prayers, and continuous inspiration. This process was not easy; despite the challenges and some limitations that came along, this book project became a success in the end.

I may not have mentioned names on this page, but to everyone who supported me in one way or another in the course of writing this book, especially those who sat through the interviews and feedback sessions; please know that I value your kindness greatly. I pray everyone who reads this book receives new insight into leading others and gains the capacity to build a cohesive team. May God continue to bless every reader of this book and my other books.

Joe Wolemonwu, DBA

FOREWORD

Every organization needs leadership. Whether you work in small enterprising entrepreneurship or a Fortune 500 conglomerate, sound leadership is required for progress. Experts will agree that effective leaders must have superior qualities, skills, and talents that influence the workforce to complete the organization's mission efficiently and effectively. Regardless, of the organization's vision and mission statement, leadership is a fundamental requirement. In this work, The *Team Lead Model Of Self Leadership,* Dr. Joe Wolemonwu offers an eight-step model that gives every leader the tools to move their agency forward.

Dr. Wolemonwu very meticulously and purposefully introduces his T.E.A.M. L.E.A.D. (Training, Enterprising, Authenticity, Mindfulness, Listening, Empathizing, Accountability, Delegation) a model that crystalizes a positive way forward for every leader. He points out that this model gives the leader credibility that people appreciate and builds trust. The author points out the importance of personal attributes and how their values transform their organization by giving reason to improve, by making the organization's success and progress enduring. In essence, this model offers a quicker rate of acceleration in all quadrants of the organization, by the consistency of the leader's conviction and commitment to excellence.

Rarely, has there been a book dedicated to growing the leader internally first, and having those qualities exhibited and passed on to the entire organization as a fundamental recipe for success and progress. Dr. Wolemonwu helps us understand, that organizations are constantly evolving, and transforming as it progresses. The same principles should apply to the leader, who must acquire new knowledge to remain relevant and effective in leading the organization. When an organization stagnates, it dies consequently failing to produce the goals of its mission. A leader must also intellectually grow, while constantly adopting and refining their personal attributes and skills which accentuate goodness and effective leadership.

    I personally and professionally appreciate the depth of this project because it should serve as both a workbook and reference manual. The author offers relevant examples and diagrams that connect with the reader by guiding you through the minefields you must navigate as you plan for success. The contours of effective leadership are unique and complex, and this self-leadership model will enhance your existing toolkit by delivering proven strategies that will do more than sustain you but will amplify your professional journey.

    Dr. Wolemonwu knocks the ball out of the park with his Team Lead model of self-leadership. The applications of this model will awaken your spirit by offering you these new behavioral paradigms, actions, and strategies that will shift your ability by becoming more effective and engaging with your workforce. When adopting the principles in this book, your workforce and staff will appreciate your improved personal involvement, marvel at your level of engagement, and be impressed with your effectiveness.

    The Team Lead Model of Self Leadership is simple to apply but requires a commitment from you to grow yourself. Pay close attention to each theory and model presented and you will surely find yourself growing and being more progressive. This is a must-read for those that are serious about becoming an effective leader. Are you that person?

– Dr. Gerald Curry, Senior Executive Service, Director, Air Force Review Boards Agency (AFRBA) at the United States Air Force.

PREFACE

The Team Lead Model framework identifies eight leadership requirements, accomplishments, and skills a leader must have to be effective. The model supports the Relational Leadership Theory of leaders concerned about their interactions with others and the process of putting people together to accomplish a change and make a difference that benefits the common good (Komives, Lucas, McMahon, 1998). The notion is that a leader must possess all the eight-core Team Lead attributes to be more effective. The Team Lead concept is a self-leadership approach to leading a team. Four attributes with the acronym T.E.A.M are *Internal* attributes the leader must possess, while the remaining four L.E.A.D show *External* attributes that enable the leader to lead the team effectively. **T.E.A.M. L.E.A.D.**

The model highlights each letter of the words "team lead." The word Team applies to the acronym T.E.A.M beginning with the letter **T-Training** enhances performance, grows knowledge, makes a leader *Competent,* and boosts productivity through learned skills. **E-Enterprising** develops a leader's capacity to generate ideas and skills that make them creatively *Resourceful.* A resourceful leader always finds a way to take advantage of a situation. **A-Authenticity** gives the leader *Credibility* and makes people appreciate your leadership. **M-Mindfulness** creates *Resilience* and happiness and increases productivity. It helps regulate your emotions. It enables you to have a greater level of emotional intelligence.

The second part of the acronym L.E.A.D begins with **L-Listening** active; listening helps a leader *Communicate* effectively and makes them more charismatic by keeping them engaged in a conversation. It helps improve the leader's relationships with others. **E-Empathizing** with others helps build *trust* and encourages open communication and effective feedback. **A-Accountability** helps to

The Team Lead Model of Self-Leadership

improve *Performance* and enables people to be in control of their actions. **D-Delegation** delegating authority helps promote *Teamwork* by creating a mentorship environment that supports learning and development with credible skills to grow and work effectively as a team.

The Team Lead Framework

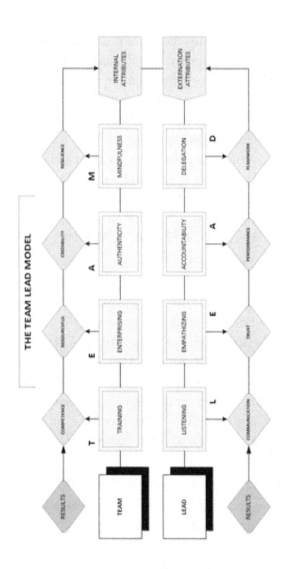

CHAPTER 1

INTRODUCTION

Learning Objectives:

- Understanding of the concept of the Team Lead Model

- Explanation of the concept of leadership and self-leadership

- The reasons for leadership failure in some organizations

- Drivers and traits of effective leadership in the workplace

- Analysis of various Self-leadership Literature

This book highlights eight attributes of effective leadership, namely Training and the ability to be teachable, Enterprising mindset, Authenticity, Mindfulness, Listening actively, Empathy, Accountability, and Delegation of authority - if you put the initials together, you get the acronym TEAM LEAD. Every effective leader has some degree of these attributes. The research conducted for this book identifies the significance of these eight attributes in the relational leadership concept and the application of the TEAM LEAD model of self-leadership, which results in effective leadership. Effective Leadership starts with self-leadership, and effective leaders have the capacity to build a cohesive team. An effective leader never tells people what to do but shows them what to do. If leaders want to bring out the best in their team, they must first bring out the best in themselves.

The TEAM LEAD Model proves that for you to be an effective leader, you must have the following eight core attributes, skills, and abilities: First, **Training** is essential for the **competency** of a leader. Having an **Enterprising mindset** helps you become resourceful as a leader, being an **Authentic** person gives you credibility as a leader, and a **mindful** person is aware of their environment and knows how to take criticism from people, which helps the person become **resilient** as a leader. Every leader must be an active **Listener** to enable them to **communicate** effectively. Also, being **Empathetic** with others will help you gain the **trust** of the people. Being **Accountable** will help you improve your **performance**. Leaders should be able to **Delegate** their authority to help promote **teamwork**. Delegating tasks to employees will empower them through mentorship and feedback. The critical point is that leaders who cannot delegate authority are usually micromanagers, and they send the wrong message to their subordinates.

What is leadership? According to Reed, Klutts, and Mattingly (2019), the most common definitions of leadership involve motivating others toward the achievement of a specific goal and leading organizational change. A leader is an individual who selects, equips, trains, and influences one or more followers who have diverse gifts, abilities, and skills and focuses the followers on the organization's mission and objectives, causing the followers to willingly and enthusiastically expend spiritual, emotional, and physical energy in a concerted coordinated effort to achieve the organizational mission and objectives (Malik, & Azmat, 2019).

What is self-leadership? Self-leadership is having a developed sense of who you are, what you can do, and where you are going, coupled with the ability to influence your communication, emotions, and behaviors on the way to getting there (Browning, 2018). Leadership is a process that begins with self-leadership (Ng, 2017). According to the scholars who first developed the theory of self-leadership, Manz, Neck, and Houghton (2016), first, learn to lead yourself, and then you will be in a solid position to effectively lead others. Most people don't like to be managed but would rather have someone lead them. Leadership is at the core of any organization's direction, and it is the primary source of any team, and its success depends on the decisions made by the leaders.

Why do organizations fail to retain productive employees? There is a reason why some organizations are very successful while others fail, and people pay attention to how successful you are in a business. Most people would love to work at a place known as the "top best places to work" because success attracts people. When a leader is successful as a result of good judgment, people want to listen to what the leader has to say, others would want to do business with them to learn their best practices or the secret to their success. Good judgment empowers a leader to make the best decisions for the team. If an organization fails or is always known for scandals, its investors will take their money elsewhere. The public always expects the leader of the organization to vacate their position when there is a scandal. It is interesting to note that whenever a scandal affects an organization, the leaders are forced to resign because of the negative impact. However, a leader's removal does not necessarily fix the issue, although, in some cases, a change in leadership can fix an issue or get to the root of the problem. Among other points, two key components of leadership failure are poor communication and lack of trust. These two make effective leadership extremely difficult. For instance, in a 2017 Federal Employee Viewpoint survey, most of the issues pointed toward the leadership were the problem of trust and communication. When there is no trust, combined with a lack of communication, it becomes impossible to lead.

Leadership is a process that begins with self-leadership (Ng, 2017).

The attributes of a successful leader using the "Team Lead" model. These attributes can help the leader effectively retain followers. It examines the impact of these leadership attributes on business success and leadership succession planning. Ineffective leadership hurts the morale of the employees and the overall job performance of an organization. This is where the TEAM LEAD model plays a critical role in solving the problem of ineffective leadership. The book will further explore the concept of "Team Lead," which is modeled toward other core leadership attributes like vision, style, and motive of a leader. The conceptual framework will support any question being addressed in this book. The research conducted during the process of writing this book showed that organizations face several leadership challenges, and the government sector is not immune to those leadership challenges, such as ineffective leadership, communication breakdown, and lack of trust and integrity. The research further showed that employees find it hard to trust their leaders, especially when there is a perceived lack of integrity. This means that when trust erodes from a leader, it becomes more difficult to regain it.

In searching through the publicly available information on "the best place to work" in the federal government and the Federal Employee Viewpoint Survey, the finding was that a particular federal agency scored one of the lowest in the best place to work in the federal government. In reviewing the historical trend, it was obvious that this same agency has been trailing at the bottom for a long time and probably will not see changes anytime soon because trust has eroded the leadership. Now the question is, how do they fix the problem of lack of trust? How do leaders develop to retain employees? Because their current employees are not motivated to remain there in the long run. What mechanisms can they put in place to help solve this leadership challenge? We've already established the fact that ineffective leadership tends to hurt the morale of the employees and the overall job performance of an organization. This research shows the **TEAM LEAD** model contributes to the leadership discourse; these attributes enable a leader to become effective by applying those qualities that make leaders efficient, thereby solving the leadership challenge. According to Nick Davis (2017) in an article "Carrer in Government" (2017), his research showed that employees lose trust in their managers when they feel in the dark, neglected, or superfluous to needs. The same research concluded that effective leadership selection is crucial to prevent bad management choices and that low levels of trust can arise as a result of a sense of injustice and a feeling of inequality. According to research conducted by the Oxford Group (2019), leadership is about relationships. The research further showed that leaders with strong, trusting, and authentic relationships with their teams recognize that investing time in building these bonds makes them more effective overall. Also, according to an article on BetterUp.com, a leader is someone who inspires passion and motivation in followers. I once read an agency (name withheld) newsletter that showed a slogan, "People First and Mission Always." This statement means that you have to care for the people in the interest of the agency's overall mission. Hence the most critical asset in the organization is the human capital. It is the human capital that you need to execute the mission. According to the Harvard Business Review (2018), people don't quit a job; they quit a boss. I once heard a leader say that supervisors should care for their subordinates. He asserted that "people leave their supervisors and not the jobs," because those same people go to another agency to do the same job they left previously. The Harvard Business Review (2018) concludes that people leave jobs, but it's up to managers to create job environments that are too good to leave.

The research for this book shows that in some organizations - both public and private - employees feel a sense of lack of leadership, seeing their leaders as simply managers. In other organizations, there is limited capacity to deal with changes from internal and external forces, sometimes resulting in leadership failure. Often the result of ineffective leadership is suboptimal objectives decided upon too late, measured with the wrong metrics, and implemented with overconfidence by a workforce that is not sufficiently empowered to deliver (Dempsey & Brafman, 2018). According to Northouse (2019), leadership is a topic with universal appeal, and despite the abundance of writing on the topic, leadership presents a major challenge to practitioners and researchers interested in understanding the nature of leadership. Research shows that for years, efforts to understand the leadership concept have focused on people in leadership roles without looking at how these challenges impact the relationship between the leader and follower. The question now is, what drives leaders to be able to build a cohesive team based on trust that will directly result in retaining those team members? We have already established that for leaders to develop or even retain followers, they must be successful at influencing people.

What are the leadership Core Drivers? There are specific core drivers in leaders that are effective. As stated earlier, the first core driver is "**Vision**." We must remember that people do not follow leaders without a vision. As a leader, it is critical to have a vision, and people will pay attention to your vision to understand where you are leading them. Another core driver is your "**Method**," which defines your leadership style or the process of executing your role as a leader. Your leadership style matters because it could determine whether you keep some followers. People may follow you initially, but when they discover that your style does not align with their values, you will lose them because they will look elsewhere for another leader who can relate to their core values and principles. Another core drive is the "**Motive**," the question of why a leader is in their current position. Why do you do the things you do? If people understand the "why," or you can convince people of your "why," they will quickly follow you because first, they believe in you and trust that you believe in the message you are sending. The core of how people are drawn to a particular leader is motive. This research examines the effect of the leader-follower relationship on retaining followers; the research intends to study how leaders can create and retain followers using the TEAM LEAD Model as well as explore the follower's perception of their leader-follower relationship

What do people want from their leaders? According to the research conducted by Stowell and Mead (2020) with over 2100 leaders for five years, including individual contributors working in various organizations such as manufacturing, entertainment, pharmaceutical, hospitality, government, and transportation. The research found that the top six desires of people from their leaders are: **1. Communication skills** - 45.2% of the people need a leader who can share vital information and cleverly engage in discourse, and the ability to listen because they want to be heard too.

2. Interpersonal skills - 44.2% of the people want leaders that can build rapport and create emotional connections with their followers.

3. Values and ethics - 41.9% of the people want their leaders to show strong values and maintain high ethical standards. The team wants to know that they can count on their leaders to do the right thing no matter the situation.

4. Personal attributes - 30.2 % shared those traits such as passion, commitment, flexibility, optimism, and accountability are very important to them in their leaders.

5. Credibility - 22.3% of the people want leaders with a high degree of competence, expertise, and experience.

6. Coaching and feedback - 21.8% of the people want leaders that can coach and develop others effectively.

What is the relevance of the TEAM LEAD Model? This research examines the eight attributes that make effective leaders and how to develop emerging leaders and retain loyal followers. This research looks at the concept of followership, what influences followership, and the core leadership drivers. There seems to be a lack of leadership and the inability to develop leaders and retain followers in the Federal Government. From the standpoint of organizations in such a turbulent environment, managers in general, and human resource managers in particular, have to ask: Do such positive beliefs matter, or is this just hollow political rhetoric? (Avey, Bruce, & Luthans, 2011). Most times, there is a misconception about management, and people often misconstrue management to be leadership. This book will help readers understand the importance of communication in effective leadership, why lack of trust persists among employees, and how to gain trust by listening to the employees. Also, this book will address the prevalent communication breakdown issue and how to build the bridge that will enhance effective communication and the challenges that arise.

The leadership processes essential to effectiveness comprise decision-making, communication, understanding human motivation, and guiding change (Chance, 2009). This research study examines the impact of various leadership attributes in retaining followers and the consequences of the leader-follower relationship related to the influence on the follower's leadership perception. We will also explore three core leadership drivers using the Team Lead model, and the intent is to clarify the blurred line between leadership and management. It is crucial to determine those traits that hinder successful leadership and why it is challenging to create and retain followers in organizations.

Analysis of Self-leadership Literature

The literature review focused on the core leadership theory with the current understanding of self-leadership before delving into the self-leadership origins and strategies. Browning (2018) described various theories and maintained that effective leaders share several typical personality characteristics. Further discussion was on the Great Man theory, Trait theory, Behavioral theory, Influence theory, and Contingency theory. This qualitative research will explore the self-leadership concept and highlight past and current literature on self-leadership. Another study supported the assertion that self-leadership considers individuals' specific traits and abilities and focuses on their behavior (Hao, Li, & Zheng, 2018). In a recent study on self-leadership, the researcher highlighted the survey conducted by Lee, Park, and Choi (2020), asserting an association between self-leadership and planning with performing an exercise; this is an intervention for improving self-leadership.

The second half of the literature review explored team-building intervention and concluded with the constructs of the study. The discussion centered on team learning and development literature focused on team training, team building, and team development (Jones, Napiersky, & Lyubovnikova, 2019). This notion means that learning and development needs have shifted from focusing solely on the individual to enhancing team effectiveness (Jones, Napiersky, & Lyubovnikova, 2019). This study discusses attributes such as authenticity, trust, teamwork, and credibility as self-leadership attributes. For this study, self-leadership is described as an individual's intrinsic motivation to influence self-regarding what, why, and how to perform tasks (Rambe, Modise, & Chipunza, 2018).

Leadership may make employees either stay or leave the organization; hence, it becomes one factor that influences employee retention (Mwita, Mwakasangula, & Tefurukwa, 2018). Leadership processes define, establish, identify, and translate this direction for their followers and facilitate or enable the organizational strategies to achieve this purpose (Mwita, Mwakasangula, & Tefurukwa, 2018). The above statement implies that leadership is an essential vehicle for helping organizations reach their intended goals and retain employees because organizations cannot survive and sustain themselves without human resources (Mwita, Mwakasangula, & Tefurukwa, 2018). Organizations invest a lot in their employees, from recruitment to selection and other human resource management functions such as compensation, training, and development (Mwita, Mwakasangula, & Tefurukwa, 2018). This assertion indicates that allowing employees to leave an organization is a costly decision for the losing organization.

Now that the significance of employee retention is established, it will be appropriate to assert that retention could benefit the organization and employees (Mwita, Mwakasangula, & Tefurukwa, 2018). The above argument supports the claim that self-leadership determines if an employee will stay within a team or leave an organization. Hence, this becomes a factor influencing employee retention (Mwita, Mwakasangula, & Tefurukwa, 2018). In considering self-leadership theory, individuals with leadership and managerial roles must ensure that employees are part and parcel of the leadership development process (Mwita, Mwakasangula, & Tefurukwa, 2018). Working as a team is not without specific challenges stemming from differences in personal backgrounds (Hurst, Arulogun, Owolabi, Akinyemi, Uvere, Warth, & Ovbiagele, 2017). This notion suggests that individuals with diverse expertise and cultural backgrounds could challenge some team members to navigate everyone's strengths and weaknesses. Hurst et al. (2017) posit that the more significant the cultural difference, the greater the potential for poor communication and misunderstanding among team members. Culture and communication could play a critical role in building a cohesive team. Understanding what each individual brings to the table through self-leadership is of more significant advantage to both the team and the organization. This section explores the comprehensive review of the self-leadership concept, core leadership theories, team-building intervention, and constructs within the study in various but comparable situations. The research discovered that the self-leadership concept is essential in team building to create teamwork in any successful organization. The literature also indicated that authenticity, credibility, trust, and teamwork are required attributes for any leader's team-building ability. Additionally, the literature revealed the importance of self-leadership in the leaders' team-building skills. The team-building intervention of the leader's attitudes towards team-building activities may provide the environment to evaluate the importance of self-leadership in team building.

The literature revealed that the inclusion and analysis of team-building intervention clarify contextual perspectives and buttresses the importance of self-leadership studies concerning the team-building abilities of a leader's behaviors. The literature provides this researcher with the opportunity to evaluate self-leadership in organizational leadership and employees' perception. Section two provides a comprehensive review of the methodology for this research study. Section two begins with a restatement of the purpose of this research study to explore the influence of self-leadership in an organization that results in authenticity, credibility, and trust, which supports team-building ability among the same leaders. This research accounts for self-leadership training opportunities for the frontline employees to grow and develop to their full potential to help with team-building skills among leaders and highlight the researcher's role. Also emphasized will be the participants' details and detailed information on the interviewees, data collection, data analysis, research design, and methodology.

Further discussed was the self-leadership perception by highlighting various self-leadership attributes such as self-assessment, self-discovery, self-acceptance, self-management, and self-development. Van Hala et al. (2018) stated that leadership self-assessment provides validation used in the collective expertise of the leaders. Nederveen Pieterse et al. (2019) provided a direct comparison of hierarchically led versus self-managing teams to draw more substantive conclusions on the impact of authority differentiation on team functioning.

Hasberry (2019) opined that self-acceptance is knowing the truth about oneself as a leader and supporting the development of others. Heizmann and Liu (2018) accentuated the need for continuing the journey of self-discovery and self-development. Zhou, Mao, and Tang (2020) argued that self-development is self-motivated and future-oriented, and it's vital for employees to self-initiate by engaging in self-development. This literature review discussed measuring self-leadership by three strategic factors: behavior-focused strategies, constructive thought patterns, and natural reward strategies. Bailey, Barber, and Justice (2018) validated the uniqueness of the self-leadership construct in self-regulation theory and determined that self-leadership is a valuable predictor of self-reported job performance beyond personality and self-regulatory traits. According to Thompson (2009), self-regulatory limitations are typical of young children whose impulsiveness, distractibility, and emotional outbursts can amuse and frustrate parents or health practitioners.

CHAPTER 2

ORIGIN OF SELF-LEADERSHIP

Learning Objectives:

- History of self-leadership

- Definition of self-leadership

- Past studies of self-leadership

- Current studies of self-leadership

- Personal leadership program

In 1986, Charles C. Manz initially presented the idea of self-leadership, and the theoretical foundation focuses on social cognitive theory, self-determination theory, and positive psychology (Neck, Manz, & Houghton, 2017). Additionally, Charles C. Manz further developed the concept with other prominent leadership scholars such as Christopher P. Neck and Jeffrey D. Houghton, who utilized this concept in other leadership theories (Neck, Manz, & Houghton, 2017). Marques (2017) discusses self-leadership from an informal stance focusing on self-regulation, self-control, and self-management. Marques (2017) emphasized the self-leadership path identified in interviews with 31 business, non-profit, and academic executives. According to Marques (2017), challenges such as altering the pace of life, unexpected change, entrepreneurial mindset, outdated habits, attitudes, and the necessity for lifetime learning, are critical to how managers perceive self-leadership.

Gannouni and Ramboarison-Lalao (2019) examined gender-role identity effects on self-perceived leadership among 371 future managers to explore the concept of self-leadership among different genders.

Gannouni and Ramboarison-Lalao (2019) compared cultural differences linked to Hofstede's masculine versus feminine countries of origin and determined no significant leadership differences between males and females. Gannouni and Ramboarison-Lalao (2019) further emphasized that masculinity and femininity correlate with leadership for males. This claim might suggest that masculinity is expressively higher for males in masculine-cultured countries, and there is a substantial connection between masculinity and organizational leadership.

Definition of self-leadership. To support the applicability of self-leadership theory, Rasdi, Hamzah, and Yean (2020) explored entrepreneurs' self-leadership development and defined self-leadership as a process developed and mastered by entrepreneurs so that they have better chances of success in their business start-ups. Rasdi, Hamzah, and Yean (2020) provided a model of the self-leadership process that illustrates a range of influences that are likely to contribute to women entrepreneurs' self-leadership development. Rasdi, Hamzah, and Yean (2020) maintained that self-leadership development is a process that includes interrelated internal and external influences. This claim means that organizations should instill attributes of the self-leadership development process among individuals who aspire to reach the top of the leadership ladder. Self-leadership is a way of intentionally influencing a thought (Bryant, 2021).

Past studies. Early research defines self-leadership as a process in which people can regulate what they do, interact with others, and decide to lead themselves and others using specific behavioral and cognitive strategies (Goldsby, Goldsby, Neck, & Neck, 2020). This idea means that self-leadership was initially a counter to how experts viewed the concept of leadership. The proponents of self-leadership focused on the leaders rather than the followers; they focused on internal factors rather than external factors. Kör (2016) suggests that self-leadership evaluates a version of the Revised Self Leadership Questionnaire (RSLQ). The RSLQ model confirms that self-leadership is effective and the measurement is good, reliable, and valid across many empirical studies (Kör, 2016). The above statement means that organizations in today's environment expect more creativity, innovation, flexible actions, collaboration, and initiation in their employees' rapidly changing conditions (Kör, 2016).

Kör's (2016) framework suggests that both leaders and employees require the opportunity to improve themselves, establish their self-management, and make decisions. Another study by Sesen, Tabak, and Arli (2017) explored the significance of self-leadership on job satisfaction, organizational commitment, and teachers' innovative behaviors. Sesen, Tabak, and Arli (2017) gathered data from 440 primary school teachers who work in different cities, showing that self-leadership behaviors substantially affected job satisfaction, organizational commitment, and innovation. Sesen, Tabak, and Arli (2017) revealed that self-reward and self-punishment strategies did not affect dependent variables, while self-observation and focusing on natural rewards had the most substantial impacts. Sesen, Tabak, and Arli (2017) argued that managers who want to incorporate self-leadership in personality trait assessment should determine whether self-leadership clarifies the unique variance in performance beyond other personality traits.

> *Early research defines self-leadership as a process in which people can regulate what they do, interact with others, and decide to lead themselves and others using specific behavioral and cognitive strategies (Goldsby et al., 2020).*

Sesen, Tabak, and Arli (2017) emphasized that self-leadership measures and defines factors such as behavior-focused strategies, constructive thought patterns, and focusing on natural rewards. Sesen, Tabak, and Arli (2017) maintained that behavior-focused strategies involve increasing awareness of one's behaviors to adapt to situational demands and improve performance. This assertion means that positive thought pattern strategies support rational thinking, increase motivation and self-efficacy, and shift challenges into opportunities. Sesen, Tabak, and Arli (2017) concluded that natural reward enhances work engagement and the task's intrinsic motivation. This concept means that focusing on natural rewards involves finding what is pleasant and rewarding about work tasks. Self-leadership requires self-reflection for monitoring situational demands and gauging the leader's reaction.

According to Koo and Park (2018), leader characteristics influence leadership styles, which cascade down from the management to the entire firm, affecting organizational and strategic outcomes. Koo and Park (2018) emphasized that the transformational leadership style's value is closely associated with a collectivist culture based on beneficial conformity virtues that are not separate from the leadership standard. Koo and Park (2018) believe that conservation may be a noticeable virtue in a positive context, increasing the influence of leadership styles. The above assertion also means that members of the public do not trust most of their political leaders. For instance, a study by Foroughi, Gabriel, and Fotaki (2019) suggested that political leaders have long been an object of suspicion in the public eye, and the collapse of trust is the critical key to the rise of post-truth politics.

Feldman's (2018) archival data indicates that articles published over the past 52 years in major international and South African journals skew the concept of leadership research. Feldman (2018) implied that leadership studies employ qualitative and mixed methodologies in their work less often than quantitative and conceptual methodologies. Feldman (2018) suggests that a need has emerged to build a followership theory that reflects the unique reality of different cultures and contexts in the global and leadership-followership environment. They relate to one another, that is, building followers' capacity that leaders understand. The study by Lacroix and Armin (2017) determined that followers' core self-evaluations and affective motivation to lead facilitated the relationship between servant leadership and reduced leadership avoidance.

Current studies. Recent research conducted by Lee, Park, and Choi (2020) defined self-leadership as a process of behavioral and cognitive self-evaluation and self-influence. This claim means that a person achieves self-direction and self-motivation to develop positive behaviors to improve their overall performance. Lee, Park, and Choi (2020) confirmed the association between self-leadership and performance measurement in their study. Another study by Bendell, Sullivan, and Marvel (2019) focused on self-leadership strategies as a cognitive resource because the nature of entrepreneurship inherently requires entrepreneurs to lead themselves as they seek to launch and grow their organizations. Bendell, Sullivan, and Marvel (2019) emphasized the importance of considering individual differences in self-leadership studies, and self-leading individuals often develop a heightened sense of ownership over their work.

An interventional study of self-leadership and action planning needs to provide specific strategies and procedures for improving self-leadership and planning. Lee, Park, and Choi (2020) determined that strategies that enhance self-leadership and action planning are essential when developing self-management intervention. Another study by Bendell, Sullivan, and Marvel (2019) focused on self-leadership strategies as a cognitive resource because the nature of entrepreneurship inherently requires entrepreneurs to lead themselves as they seek to launch and grow their organizations. In their study, Bendell, Sullivan, and Marvel (2019) emphasized the importance of considering individual differences in self-leadership studies. Bendell, Sullivan, and Marvel (2019) focused on self-leadership theory, gender, and entrepreneurship. Bendell, Sullivan, and Marvel (2019) suggested that some self-leadership strategies are helpful when applied to high-growth entrepreneurship. This concept means that the advanced gender-aware framework of self-leadership strategies supports high growth in organizations. Bendell, Sullivan, and Marvel (2019) asserted that self-leading individuals often develop a heightened sense of ownership over their work and exhibit a more substantial commitment to their goals, tasks, or organization.

Bendell, Sullivan, and Marvel (2019) argued that self-leadership helps the gender-aware framework associated with high-growth entrepreneurs. The above viewpoint also means that both men and women differently emphasized self-leadership approaches and realized varying outcomes to the applicability. Bendell, Sullivan, and Marvel

(2019) further suggested integrating and considering individual differences will be prudent to study self-leadership. Bendell, Sullivan, and Marvel (2019) argued that self-leading individuals tend to be opportunity thinkers who challenge prevailing assumptions and attitudes. Bendell, Sullivan, and Marvel (2019) concluded that there had been a great deal of self-leadership research to date and that much has been conceptual and focused on managers and teams in organizational settings. This claim means that given the potential value of self-leadership for entrepreneurs, who inherently require self-direction, the lack of empirical studies focusing on employees, the concept of self-leadership and organizations is astounding.

Personal Leadership Program. Another study conducted by Roberts, Fawcett, and Searle (2019) evaluated a high school's effectiveness based on a Personal Leadership Program designed to promote positive social, emotional and motivational outcomes. Roberts, Fawcett, and Searle (2019) demonstrated improvements in positive functioning across a range of measures of wellbeing. According to Roberts, Fawcett, and Searle (2019), the Personal Leadership Program is a primary prevention program that supports adolescent participants who choose to take control of their lives by deciding to be happy, set goals, think, and communicate positive messages. This notion means that personal or self-leadership is about individual responsibility and personal choice and that individuals can choose to take control of their lives. Roberts, Fawcett, and Searle (2019) concluded that Personal Leadership Program participants experienced a medium to a significant increase in goal-setting and self-esteem measures relative to the comparison group.

Further study suggests that self-leadership requires self-reflection for monitoring, both for comparing performance to situational demands and gauging one's reaction (Bailey, Barber, & Justice, 2018). This same study argues that monitoring behaviors can help individuals determine necessary improvements and guide their performance towards improvement (Bailey, Barber, & Justice, 2018). Self-leadership assesses specific self-regulatory tendencies that help predict workplace performance consistently across aspects of self-reported job performance (Bailey, Barber, & Justice, 2018). Self-leadership is indicative of traits related to diligence, an understanding of situational demands, and self-awareness in the work context (Bailey, Barber, & Justice, 2018). Self-leadership training must incorporate the TEAM LEAD framework discussed in the previous chapter: competence, resourcefulness, credibility, resilience, effective communication, trust, job performance, and teamwork.

By emphasizing self-leadership, organizations could accentuate the motivation-related personality and self-regulatory traits in a way that is practical and relevant to their individual, team, and organizational performance contexts (Bailey, Barber, & Justice, 2018). The research concluded that self-leadership is related to self-regulation uniquely from personality and is more than just personality and self-regulation when predicting self-reported job performance. The study by Marvel and Patel (2018) highlighted self-leadership as a critical behavioral and motivational resource for speeding product development in the new technology-based venture context. Marvel and Patel (2018) shed light on the value of self-leadership in accelerating the development of less radical or incremental product innovations. Marvel and Patel (2018) stated that the research findings had implications for entrepreneurship research and self-leadership literature.

Marvel and Patel (2018) emphasized that self-leadership could be a critical resource under the time constraints of product launch. They further stated that self-leadership is a form of individual leadership that closely represents the cognitive and behavioral elements that drive innovation efforts despite resource constraints or organizational routines to draw on. Marvel and Patel (2018) determined that self-leadership has roots in several related theories of self-influence, including self-regulation, self-control, self-management, and intrinsic motivation. Self-leadership prescribes specific sets of behavioral and cognitive elements of value to individual performance outcomes. Marvel and Patel (2018) highlighted the significance of self-leadership to accelerate less radical product innovation. The research concludes that self-leadership fast-tracks innovation and helps in economic development to recognize the cognitive aspects of leaders' significance in the selection or coaching efforts. This claim means applying a self-leadership strategy will quicken invention and creativity within the workforce. Applying the TEAM LEAD model will help leaders become more resourceful, credible, and resilient.

According to Bäcklander, Rosengren, and Kaulio (2018), self-leadership theory suggests that behavior is ultimately internal and individually controlled even though there could be other significant influences such as external leadership and other forces. To ascertain the theory, Bäcklander, Rosengren, and Kaulio (2018) interviewed a group of management consultants in a Danish management consultancy firm. Bäcklander, Rosengren, and Kaulio (2018) argued that the framework for self-leading strategies develops the dimensions of reactive/proactive and self-focused/externally focused strategies in different combinations. This claim could mean that as leaders support internal self-discipline strategies of a more reactive nature, external and proactive strategies endorse the most effective practice. Dewan and Squintani (2018) emphasized that a leader takes a decision on behalf of the organization, and that good leadership depends on moderation and judgment characteristics. Dewan and Squintani's (2018) analysis relates features that define good leadership, such as moderation, judgment, and communication structure. Dewan and Squintani (2018) believe the role of judgment could relate to the leader's trustworthy associates.

> *Self Leadership is an enabling process whereby a person learns to know him/herself better and through this better self-understanding is able to steer his/her life better*
>
> **Joshi, 2021**

CHAPTER 3

CORE LEADERSHIP THEORY

Learning Objectives:

- The Great man theory

- Behavioral/Trait theory

- Influence theory

- Relational theory

- Contingency theory

Most leadership's success thrives on having a good vision, leveraging unwavering energy and passion, and focusing on a positive path. Most significantly, motivating people to convey trust, contribute to the team's effort, and work together to attain a set goal will help organizations retain employees (Browning, 2018). This claim means that core leadership theories support the current understanding of leadership before exploring the self-leadership concept. For instance, positive effects on the followers' contributions will result in leadership success (Buchholz, & Sandler, 2017). According to Browning (2018), trait theories suggest that effective leaders share many typical personality characteristics. The early trait theories view leadership as an innate, instinctive quality of individuals. The theory identifies qualities such as integrity, empathy, and assertiveness as helpful traits for leading others. However, Williams and Lowman (2018) argued that neither these traits nor any specific combination guarantee success as a leader. Williams and Lowman (2018) maintained that a leader should inspire others to do tasks without close supervision instead of micro-managing the subordinates. This idea could mean that the leader is growing in their leadership competencies and behaviors rather than controlling employees without allowing them to work as individuals.

Another core leadership theory is behavioral and contingency or situational theories. The behavioral theories focus on how leaders behave, while the contingency or situational approach's fundamental component is that the organization or workgroup affects the extent to which, if given, a leader's traits and behaviors will be effective (Browning, 2018). The fourth core leadership theories are the power and influence theory. These theories focus on the source of the leader's power, based on the different ways that leaders use influence to get things done (Browning, 2018). A leader should use influence to inspire others to do tasks without subordinates' micro-management (Williams & Lowman, 2018). This assertion means that there is growth in the leader's behaviors for coaching employees rather than controlling them through the disguise of close supervision. Hunt and Weintraub (2017) suggested that appropriately applying the concept of coaching can help create better relationships between managers and employees. Coaching shows that when a leader takes on a mentor's role through training, there is essentially growth for employees and their success.

Organizations may involve individual leadership coaches, while some require coaches to work with individual employees (Hunt & Weintraub, 2017). This notion means that these leaders may need a coach when they begin a new career or accept a leadership position in an existing one (Hunt & Weintraub, 2017). Organizational leaders should be clear about the value of different leadership development options and the likely impact of each (Gavin, 2018). This claim means that organizations should consider other leadership development options such as self-directed, management-prompted, and coaching. The study conducted by Sigrid and Weibler Jürgen (2020) determined that the context of taking the lead implies shifting leadership understanding from the general individual-centered leadership understanding to a collective and identity-based view of leadership.

Sigrid and Weibler Jürgen (2020) believe that individuals become in some way empowered by their network-specific embeddedness and feel a particular aversion to traditional single leadership. Eide, Saether, and Aspelund (2020) agree that leaders with a personal motivation for sustainability are more likely to lead firms with sustainability strategies. However, Eide, Saether, and Aspelund (2020) suggest that firms' strategic positioning on sustainability influences the managers' motivation and way of leading their employees. Eide, Saether, and Aspelund (2020) found that top managers perceive sustainability strategies as associated with higher value creation and solving significant challenges. This statement means that leaders view sustainability strategy as a tool that benefits organizations and helps in problem-solving and decision-making.

> *Organizational leaders should be clear about the value of different leadership development options and the likely impact of each (Gavin, 2018).*

The Great Man theory. The great man theory is one of the oldest leadership theories. According to Mouton (2019), Carlyle first codified the Great Man leadership theory in 1841. Mouton (2019) argued that the theory is popular among scholars and thrives among practitioners. In politics, the Great Man theory's myth still seems to shape the minds of many politicians, citizens, and political commentators. Mouton (2019) asserted that this theory views leaders as influential geniuses capable of creating comprehensive plans that predict all contingencies and control incredibly intricate rigorous actions. Rüzgar (2019) claimed that the Great Man Theory's longevity is the oldest approach to several leadership types of research. Rüzgar (2019) argued that the theory goes back to ancient Greek times; among the early supporters of the theory, Herodot and Tacitus focused on great leaders and tried to unravel the traits that differentiated them from the others.

The above statement connotes that this theory's proponents' common viewpoint is that an individual should have some innate traits to become a great leader. Rüzgar (2019) suggests that great men influence people and have power over them and those great men who possess particular inborn and God-given talents shaped human history.

These traits are impossible to obtain later in life by mere experience. This assertion means that great men were known as liberators, inventors, and heroes during their era. These leaders sometimes emerged to satisfy needs, which shaped social, economic, and moral feelings. Rüzgar (2019) determined that these leaders' strong characteristics and personalities show a superior talent to lead a supportive society. The theory of these leaders who hold certain superior traits should agree with the group or society's needs.

Trait theory. Trait theories argue that effective leaders share many common personality characteristics or traits. Early trait theories said that leadership is innate, instinctive quality individuals do or do not have. None of these traits, nor any specific combination of them, guarantee success as a leader (Browning, 2018). However, trait theories do aid in identifying traits and qualities such as integrity, empathy, and assertiveness that are helpful when leading others (Browning, 2018). Another study explored academics' experiences in higher education institutions and their self-leadership traits in an educational environment (Jooste & Frantz, 2017). The study was known as Cashman's theoretical framework of seven pathways for an academic and considered relevant to the specific concept of self-leadership and the context of academics in this study, focusing on leading from the inside out (Jooste & Frantz, 2017).

The trait theory of leadership suggests that certain individuals possess specific traits (Wyatt & Silvester, 2018). Some traits lead observers to ascribe competence and infer suitability for leadership. These may not be the same as those traits that influence leaders' effectiveness once in a role (Wyatt & Silvester, 2018). A previous study suggested that happy emotions result in higher leadership ratings, higher trait ratings, more significant correlations among trait ratings, and greater dependence of trait ratings on leadership perceptions (Trichas, Schyns, Lord, & Hall, 2017). An exploratory model suggested that leadership impressions mediated facial emotions' effects on trait ratings (Trichas et al., 2017). The emotions displayed by leaders affected perceivers' leadership and trait perceptions, the covariances among trait perceptions, and the extent to which trait perceptions were associated with overall leadership impressions (Trichas et al., 2017). Patterns of traits are simply from brief exposure to leaders' faces, but this process mediates the leadership perception (Trichas et al., 2017).

Behavioral theory. The behavioral theory explores three types of leaders: autocratic, democratic, and laissez-faire leaders. Browning (2018) suggested that autocratic leaders decide without consulting their teams, and this leadership style is appropriate when decisions need to be quick. The above viewpoint means that there is no need for input, and the team does not require everybody's agreement for a successful outcome. According to Buchholz and Sandler (2017), positive effects on the followers' public good contributions may result in the leadership's success, which in theoretical terms means that the follower's reaction path is upward sloping. Buchholz and Sandler (2017) further reviewed the existing academic literature on the effects of leaders' behavior on followers going beyond the good public model.

Fingleton, Duncan, Watson, and Matheson (2019) suggest that behavioral theory is a tool that predicts or generates behavior change in individuals. Fingleton et al. (2019) state that capability, opportunity, and motivation represent the behavioral model theory. This statement means that the linked theoretical domains framework explores perceived influences on the behavior of the leader. Fingleton et al. (2019) maintain that the theoretical domains framework provides a comprehensive framework to prompt identifying factors that influence behavior, and consequently, potential mediators of behavior change. This assertion could also mean that this theoretical domain framework is a critical component that leads to the change in organizational leaders' behavior that applies to self-leadership.

Contingency theory. The fourth of the core leadership theories is the contingency approach. Browning (2018) suggested that the fundamental component of a contingency leader is that the organization or the team affects the extent to which given leader traits and behaviors will be effective. Browning (2018) emphasized that contingency theories gained prominence in the late 1960s and 1970s. Fiedler's contingency theory, path-goal theory, the Vroom-Yetton-Jago decision-making leadership model, and situational leadership theory are four well-known contingency theories. According to Vidal,

Campdesuñer, Rodríguez, and Vivar (2017), the contingency leadership theory assumes that leadership characteristics significantly depend on circumstantial factors. Furlan Matos Alves, Lopes de Sousa Jabbour, Kannan, and Chiappetta Jabbour (2017) further defined contingencies as outside events that affect organizations.

Furlan Matos Alves et al. (2017) determined for sure that organizations might already face or will potentially face an unpredictable situation. This claim means that good leaders always step up and create contingencies for any case or circumstance. According to Moreno-Gómez and Calleja-Blanco (2018), the contingency theory of leadership underscores a leader's personality and the situation in which a leader operates to influence corporate decision-making. Moreno-Gómez and Calleja-Blanco (2018) suggested that leadership's contingency theory in organizational performance has positive effects.

Influence theory. The influence theories suggest that the source of the leader's power is based on how leaders use power and influence to get things done (Browning, 2018). Influence is the capacity to have an effect on the character, behavior development, or behavior of someone or something or the effect itself. This idea means that influence impacts the behaviors, attitudes, opinions, and choices of other people. On the other hand, influence should not be confused with power or control, and one of the best-known theories is the French and Raven's five forms of power (Browning, 2018). The research emphasized that the present study has enriched our theoretical understanding of how goal-focused leadership influences followers (Qian, Li, Wang, Song, Zhang, Chen, & Qu, 2018). Another study suggested that self-leadership could influence team engagements (Kotzé, 2018). Hence, organizations can better develop and master self-leadership to succeed (Rasdi, Hamzah, & Yean, 2020).

Relational theory: The relationship is built through interpersonal exchanges in which parties to the relationship evaluate the ability, benevolence, and integrity, and these perceptions, in turn, influence the behaviors. (Brower, Schoorman, & Tan, 2000). Social influence develops new approaches, values, attitudes, behaviors, and ideologies (Uhl-Bien, 2006). Relational leaders are concerned about their interactions with others and the process of putting people together to accomplish a change and make a difference that benefits the common good (Komives, Lucas, McMahon, 1998). Relational leaders mentor their employees through regular interaction and effective communication.

CHAPTER 4

THE TEAM LEAD MODEL

Learning Objectives:

- The theoretical and conceptual framework
- Understanding of the TEAM internal constructs
- Understanding of the LEAD external constructs
- Enhancing the eight leadership attributes
- The process of building a cohesive team

T.E.A.M.	Train	Enterprising	Authentic	Mindful
L.E.A.D.	Listen	Empathy	Accountable	Delegate

*Table 1. Theoretical **TEAM LEAD** Model – Attributes*

Theoretical Framework - the focus of this theory is basically to highlight the impact of self-leadership on effective leadership in the application of the TEAM LEAD model. The term 'self-leadership' first emerged from organizational management literature by Charles C. Manz in 1983, who later defined it as a "comprehensive self-influence perspective that concerns leading oneself toward the performance of naturally motivating tasks as well as managing oneself to do work that must be done but is not naturally motivating" (Manz, 1986). In researching self-leadership theories, overall, I discovered that there are a limited amount of self-leadership models and guiding frameworks in existence, coupled with limited data on the historical development of the scientific self-leadership evidence. The Team Lead Model explicitly combines eight self-leadership traits with relational leadership theory from both self-leadership and leadership literature. The importance of self-leadership in the context of the leader's team-building ability will help leaders improve individual and organizational performance (Browning, 2018). This model is based on an expanded theory of self-influence processes in organizations (Manz, 1996). It aligns with leaders' experiences in delivering team-building interventions regarding positive self-leadership development. It offers several competencies (internal constructs) across four dynamically interacting core capabilities such as being teachable, having an enterprising mindset, credibility, and emotional intelligence (external constructs): listening, empathy, accountability, and delegation of authority (Ramamoorthi et al., 2021). Emotionally intelligent leaders have strong verbal ability and reasoning that enhances effective self-leadership, thus making emotional intelligence an important leadership trait (Daud, 2020). Self-awareness is the starting point of effective and authentic leadership, which enhances individual effectiveness and performance (Daud, 2020).

Relational leadership supports being open to differences, undergoing cognitive shifts through framing and reframing, building coalitions, listening, encouraging others, and promoting a sense of self-leadership (Ramamoorthi et al., 2021). The main dimension of empowerment is the sense of self-leadership felt by an individual who claims a place in the group process (Komives et al., 1998). This research shows that applying self-leadership broadens team members' contributions to the team in working towards the shared goal (Ramamoorthi et al., 2021). This framework on page 27 shows the relationship between the leadership attributes and their impact resulting in effective leadership by applying the TEAM LEAD model. It examines the impact of the core self-leadership drivers on the TEAM LEAD model. The conceptual framework shows the blueprint of this model. The TEAM LEAD model leverages various self-leadership attributes as drivers for effective leadership, which ultimately impacts the leader's effectiveness through the result shown in the framework. The TEAM LEAD model shows that there are three core drivers, which are: vision resulting in the creation of "value," motive resulting in the building of "loyalty," and method which results in "acceptance." These core drivers ask the question: "What?" for vision, "why?" for motive, and "how?" for method. To better understand this model, this book highlights examples of people that were effective leaders and how they applied the concept of self-leadership to remain relevant.

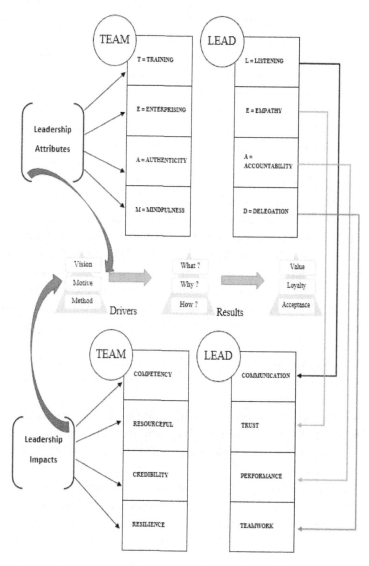

Figure 1. *The conceptual framework for TEAM LEAD*

THE INTERNAL CONSTRUCT (T.E.A.M.)

The (T) connotes Training. Training enhances an individual's performance, boosts employee productivity, reduces overall turnover, and improves organizational culture. It is critical that leaders continuously explore the benefits of training and development programs for employees. Employers must pursue the idea of developing their employees for the success of the organization. Leadership training provides feedback and insight on the positive aspects of the leader's actions and styles. Leadership training programs ensure those strengths are explored and mastered, building a well-rounded and effective mentorship program in the workplace. The **TEAM LEAD** model shows that **Training** helps leaders become more **Competent**. Highly competent leaders do more than perform at a high level; they inspire and motivate their followers to do the same. While some individuals rely on relational skills alone to survive, effective leaders combine these skills with high competence to take their organizations to a new level of excellence and influence.

In accordance with Clause 7.5 of the ISO 9001:2018, it's vital to maintain evidence of continuing competence as documented information. An organization should define competency requirements by actively identifying training requirements, delivering training, and monitoring training effectiveness. Training should never be performed without real objectives and thinking it through; instead, it should be focused on empowering each employee with the skills and knowledge they need to move the organization forward and enhance leaders' performance. Training alone is not sufficient to demonstrate competence; this must be shown through feedback, observations, and results produced by the leader who participated in the training.

Great leaders have long understood that leadership and learning are inseparably connected – it will be challenging to have one without the other. According to John F. Kennedy, 35th President of the United States, "leadership and learning are indispensable to each other." Peter Drucker, American management consultant, educator, and author, says, "We now accept the fact that learning is a lifelong process of keeping abreast of change. And the most pressing task is to teach people how to learn." Peter M. Senge, in The Fifth Discipline: The Art and Practice of the Learning Organization, says, "real learning gets to the heart of what it means to be human. Through learning, we re-create ourselves. Through learning, we become able to do something we never were able to do. Through learning, we reperceive the world and our relationship to it. Through learning, we extend our capacity to create and be part of life's generative process. There is within each of us a deep hunger for this type of learning." Mr. Bill Gates, Microsoft founder, and philanthropist believes that once you embrace unpleasant news not as negative but as evidence of a need for change, you're learning from it.

The (E) connotes Enterprising. An enterprising leader works with people, influence, persuade, lead or manage for organizational goals or economic gain. An enterprising personality type is often a leader who is talented at organizing, persuading, and managing. They are practical, quick thinking, imaginative, inventive, innovative, creative-minded, and always take the lead wherever they find themselves. According to an article by CareerKey in 2021, "Enterprising" leaders create an "Enterprising" environment. For example, they particularly value energetic, ambitious, and friendly people who are good at politics, leading people, and selling things or ideas. The TEAM LEAD model of self-leadership shows that, in general term, a highly enterprising person has the following qualities: very **Resourceful**, have a strong need for achievement; like to be in charge; seek opportunities and use resources to achieve plans; believe that they possess or can gain the qualities to be successful; are innovative and willing to take calculated risks to ensure that the organization succeeds.

Enterprising leaders can resourcefully work through a crisis and keep things moving forward. Resourcefulness is seeing the obstacles, coming up with solutions, overcoming the problem, and moving towards the goal. An example that comes to mind is the Biblical illustration of the enterprising mindset and the resourcefulness of Nehemiah. The Bible highlights Nehemiah's resourcefulness in rebuilding Jerusalem's wall (Nehemiah 1:1-7,73; Nehemiah 4). It took Nehemiah 52 days to reinforce the gaps and rebuild the wall. He gathered his people together, equipped them, and led them in rebuilding the city walls of Jerusalem. After the wall was built, Nehemiah ensured that the people read God's Law and understood it. The people were focused on the goal; the wall was being joined together. The people had a mind to work. On the external view, the pessimists and adversaries became very angry at the progress, to the point of plotting together to fight and disrupt God's plan for them. The man Nehemiah discussed in this chapter was resourceful, and resourceful leaders are self-leaders.

> The concept of self-leadership is explained and summarized in 1 Timothy 3: 1 -7(New International Version), which says "Here is a trustworthy saying: Whoever aspires to be an overseer desires a noble task. [2]Now the overseer is to be above reproach, faithful to his wife, temperate, self-controlled, respectable, hospitable, able to teach, [3]not given to drunkenness, not violent but gentle, not quarrelsome, not a lover of money. [4]He must manage his own family well and see that his children obey him, and he must do so in a manner worthy of full[a] respect. [5](If anyone does not know how to manage his own family, how can he take care of God's church?) [6]He must not be a recent convert, or he may become conceited and fall under the same judgment as the devil. [7]He must also have a good reputation with outsiders so that he will not fall into disgrace and into the devil's trap."

The above Biblical perspective explains some qualities of a self-leader and offers a solution to the lack of self-leadership by addressing the attributes effective leaders should have before leading others. The process of conducting business from a Biblical perspective is a relevant discussion in the sense that it resonates with me as a person of faith, and to apply these moral principles in my professional practice.

Another example of a resourceful leader is Walt Disney. During his formative years, in the lead-up to World War II, Disney built the beginnings of his empire based mostly on Participative leadership, but he was extremely resourceful. In the late 1930s, after the incredible success of Snow White, Disney was building an enormous studio complex in Burbank, CA. He needed to find and hire more than 700 skilled artists, often traveling the country to recruit them. Because he was resourceful, he gave incentives by even offering to sponsor their education to help improve their skills. To generate a single story required tens of thousands of hours of artistic input, which meant mastering the job of resourceful leaders.

The (A) connotes Authenticity. The TEAM LEAD model shows that authenticity results in **Credibility.** The Center for Creative Leadership believes that authentic individuals bring their whole selves to their jobs and participate fully and honestly in the workplace. According to YSCOUTS (2021), authentic leadership works on the principle that leaders can prove their legitimacy by nurturing sincere relationships with their subordinates and giving importance to their input. Authentic leader encourages their subordinates to be more open; they appreciate their support in the organization's success.

We have observed various authentic leadership instances throughout history: Mr. Mahatma Karamchand Gandhi, a notable Indian lawyer; President Nelson Rolihlahla Mandela, a freedom fighter and former South African President; and Dr. Martin Luther King Jr., a civil rights activist. These individuals listed are renowned authentic leaders. They all endeavored for the progress of their people and made every possible effort to achieve their objectives by being authentic. Mr. Gandhi is indeed a genuine, passionate, and trustworthy leader who led India to freedom. In my view, Gandhi is an excellent example of an individual who exhibited authentic leadership. Mr. Gandhi created the Satyagraha movement in India, which translates to "insistence upon truth."

President Nelson Mandela created a whole new world for everyone by consistently being an authentic leader and driven by democratic principles (PennState, 2022). At the time of his struggle, these principles seemed impossible to many; nevertheless, he was able to get people to adopt his vision of the world, especially in Africa. Martin Luther King Jr. is another example of an authentic leader who built an honest, trustworthy relationship with his followers (Jing, 2021). Dr. King most times was outspoken when discriminated against, despite constantly running into problems while being authentic. Dr. King's self-confidence and passion inspired and gave others the courage to be fearless leaders, especially by putting himself in danger many times. Authentic leadership can be summarized as an individual's beliefs and values, how those beliefs and values influence them to process and get through critical life events, and how that, in turn, shapes the relationships they form. For this to happen, the individual must thus acquire moral reasoning and positive ethical values.

The (M) connotes Mindfulness. In a Forbes Magazine article (2019) on "how to develop Emotional Intelligence using Mindfulness," they described mindfulness as a vital tool in understanding ourselves, our thoughts and feelings, and what is important to us. It can help you develop self-awareness, which is the first component of emotional intelligence and is the basis for developing other emotional intelligence skills. According to the Harvard Gazette (2021), mindfulness teaches you the skill of paying attention to the present by noticing when your mind wanders off. Mindfulness is the essential human ability to be fully present, aware of where we are and what we're doing, and not overly reactive. Mindfulness encompasses two crucial ingredients: awareness and acceptance. Awareness is the knowledge and ability to focus attention on one's inner processes and experiences, such as the experience of the present moment. Acceptance is the ability to observe and accept those streams of thought rather than judge or avoid them. The TEAM LEAD model shows that mindfulness results in **Resilience**.

Resilient leaders can sustain their energy level under pressure, cope with disruptive changes, and adapt. They bounce back from setbacks. They also overcome significant difficulties without engaging in dysfunctional behavior or harming others. For instance, Ludwig Van Beethoven composed five of his famous symphonies while he was completely deaf. President Franklin D. Roosevelt was partially paralyzed when he was 39 years old and still became one of the most respected American presidents. President Nelson Mandela spent 27 years in prison for political offenses and still made it as one of the most iconic World leaders. Albert Einstein couldn't talk until four years old, couldn't read until seven years old, and was expelled from school, but we know him today as the modern synonym of genius. Frederick Douglass went from being a slave to becoming a well-known writer and activist and even advisor to the president. Winston Churchill failed twice the military academy exams and lost elections five times to become the man we know today. Churchill is best remembered for successfully leading Britain through World War II. Mindful leaders can personally separate themselves from stressful events. They learn not to take organizational pressures personally and observe situations from a neutral position. This mindset makes them resilient as leaders.

THE EXTERNAL CONSTRUCT (L.E.A.D.)

The (L) connotes Listening – The TEAM LEAD model of self-leadership shows that active listening encourages more robust **communication** between leaders and their team members. Listening increases the capacity of a leader to communicate effectively. Employees who feel their leaders listen are more likely to speak up and share their ideas and perspectives. Leaders who develop their listening skills can help boost an organization's culture of profound listening. One of the most important skills a leader can master is the ability to listen. According to Peter Drucker, "the most important thing in communication is to hear what isn't being said." Dr. Misner from the University of Southern California, a New York Times Bestselling author who has written 26 books, including one of his latest books, "Who's in Your Room?" agrees with Peter Drucker and states that the quality of our relationships depends on the quality of our communications. Active listening shows engagement. It shows that the leader cares and is open to new ideas, constructive criticism, and building relationships. Listening shows respect and regard for the people in the workplace. When a leader listens, that leader can build rapport with people. Richard Branson, the founder of the Virgin Group, is arguably the king of all listening leaders. Mr. Branson summed up his success as a leader in five simple words: "Listen more than you talk.' Recognizing that nobody learns anything by listening to themselves speak, Mr. Branson's belief in listening as a critical soft skill is encouraged across all Virgin brands.

The prime minister of New Zealand, Jacinda Ardern, was lauded for her decisive response to the Coronavirus pandemic among several other world leaders. When leaders and scientists overseas painted a bleak picture of the impending spread of the virus, Jacinda Ardern listened. On his first day as CEO of Tesco, Mr. Dave Lewis sent a message to every employee asking them how they thought the declining business could be improved. Almost half a million employees were encouraged to email back with ideas and suggestions. Mr. Dave Lewis said, "I will always communicate openly and transparently with you, and I'd like to encourage the same from you in return. I want to hear your thoughts and ideas. I want to hear what you think we could do differently or better." Ms. Sheryl Sandberg, the Facebook Chief Operations Officer and the author of the New York Times best-seller, 'Lean In,' understands the significance of being a better leader by being open to feedback. Ms. Sandberg regularly asks, "what could I do better?" and often commends them publicly for voicing honest opinions.

The (E) connotes Empathy. The TEAM LEAD model shows that being empathetic allows leaders to help struggling employees improve and excel. Empathy will enable leaders to build and develop relationships of **trust** with those they lead. An empathetic leader can lead while understanding the contexts, experiences, and needs of others and being aware of their thoughts and feelings. An empathetic leader can live and experience the story of another as if it were their own. According to an article by Tanveer Naseer (2021), empathy allows us to feel safe with our failures because we won't simply be blamed for them. Empathy could help establish trust because it is a key to strong relationships, and it allows employees to develop trusting relationships (Rahman, 2016). Empathy gives employees the ability to place themselves in other people's shoes and understand their feelings, allowing them to work together as a team (Rahman, 2016).

There are leaders in our history who led by showing empathy, and the first example I will share is Saint Francis of Assisi, whose birth name was Giovanni Bernadone. In 1206, Saint Francis, a 23-year-old son of a wealthy merchant, went on a pilgrimage to St. Peter's Basilica in Rome. He could not help noticing the contrast between the wealth and luxury within the brilliant mosaics, the spiral columns, and the poverty of the beggars sitting outside. He persuaded one of them to exchange clothes with him and spent the rest of the day in rags begging for alms. It was one of the first great empathy experiments in human history. Another is the story of Beatrice Webb, born in 1858 into a family of well-off businessmen and politicians. However, in 1887, as part of her research into urban poverty, she stepped out of her comfortable bourgeois life. She dressed up in a bedraggled skirt and buttonless boots to work in an East London textile factory. The account of her adventure, Pages from a Work-Girl's Diary, caused a sensation. It was unheard of for a member of respectable society, especially a woman, to have firsthand experience of life among the destitute. Lastly was former U.S. President Barack Obama, who showed empathy by crying seven times throughout his presidency. On a specific occasion was during his speech on gun violence in the U.S.A. He said he got "upset" when he thought about "those kids" killed by gun violence.

The (A) connotes Accountability. The TEAM LEAD model shows that accountability helps with a leader's **performance**. Accountability is accepting responsibility for your actions and being willing to own the outcomes of your choices, decisions, and actions. When leaders take personal accountability, they are willing to answer for the outcomes of their choices, behaviors, and actions. According to the center for creative leadership, "if you want accountable leaders, you need to create the conditions that encourage people to own their decisions fully." Great business leaders understand that acceptance of greater personal accountability and responsibility leads individuals, teams, and organizations back on the path to success (Worrall, 2013). Many organizations have seen temporary improvements, implementing traditional accountability systems to drive high **performance** in the workplace—only to quickly revert to their old ways or worse (Worrall, 2013).

In American history, some leaders showed accountability, and one of them was President Teddy Roosevelt. He believed in taking personal responsibility for acknowledging things about yourself that get in the way of your performance and the adequate performance of others. "If you could kick the person in the pants most responsible for most of your trouble, you wouldn't sit for a month." He remains the youngest person to become President of the United States. Roosevelt was a leader of the progressive movement, and he championed his "Square Deal" domestic policies, promising the average citizen fairness, trust, regulation of railroads, and quality food and drugs. President Harry Truman took Teddy Roosevelt's notion further, living by the belief that he couldn't pass the buck to anyone else when it came to taking responsibility for the way the country was governed – this from a man who ordered that the atomic bomb be dropped on Hiroshima and Nagasaki. "The buck stops here." Truman led the United States through the final stages of World War II and the early years of the Cold War, vigorously opposing Soviet expansionism in Europe. According to Rapaport (2017), another accountable leader was Ms. Eleanor Roosevelt. She held the belief that there is a very concrete connection between "choices" and "accountability." In Eleanor Roosevelt's worldview, the choice was clear – to accept responsibility for choosing good over evil (Rapaport, 2017).

The (D) connotes Delegation. The TEAM LEAD model shows that delegation of authority helps to promote teamwork. Delegation of authority helps both supervisors and subordinates. Delegation can help others develop or enhance their skills, promote teamwork, and improve productivity through **mentorship**. Delegating responsibilities to team members helps utilize the capabilities and strengths of other individuals within the organization. According to Wood Personnel Services, when a leader assigns a project to a group, the group depends upon one another to achieve whatever goal they've set. By transferring responsibility to them collectively, the leader helps employees focus less on their job and more on working together to reach the bigger goal. Effective leaders know how to delegate without micromanaging.

Another example is in the book of Joshua 18:3 (NIV), which says: "So, Joshua said to the Israelites, 'how long may you put off going in to take possession of the land, which the LORD, the God of your ancestors, has given you? Appoint three men from each tribe, and I will send them out to make a survey of the land and write the description of it, according to the inheritance of each. Then they may return to me."

Joshua showed effective leadership by understanding the inequity faced by the people of Israel in their inheritance, so he decided to lead by delegating the task to three men from each tribe. The men did as they were told and mapped the entire territory into seven sections, listing the towns in each area. They made a written record and then returned to Joshua in the camp at Shiloh" (Joshua 18:3-4, 9, NLT). Joshua sent the three on a fact-finding mission, and they reported their findings to their leader, giving him data on how to distribute the land among them equitably. Joshua led effectively by distributing the land to the children of Israel according to their tribes. Joshua fulfilled the leadership requirement of effective team building by selecting the three men to conduct the survey. In this research, I selected a team of participants by identifying people who have first-hand information on the role of leadership in the employee's decision to leave or stay at their current employment. By serving as participants, they will contribute to the growth and development of the working environment in the organization. As we previously discussed in the book of Joshua, the three men's participation in the survey of the land and providing the reports of their study to Joshua made it possible for him to make an informed decision on how to distribute the land to the children of Israel. In the case of the children of Israel, the purpose was to inform an action since the people were requesting for the land to be distributed and to have the correct information. Joshua built a team of three men to research by surveying the land and reporting back to the children of Israel with Joshua as the leader.

The assumption is that Joshua intended to get the facts by sending these men to conduct a survey and map out the land. Joshua exemplified self-leadership by applying the enterprising mindset and creating practical goals that align with the TEAM LEAD framework of self-leadership, helping the team to meet their highest priorities of attending to the needs of the children of Israel. According to the Bible, in the book of Joshua 18, the men went on a fact-finding mission by visiting various landscapes and documenting the evidence for Joshua to use in his decision-making. On arrival, all three men reported their findings to

Joshua, who used the information to distribute the land according to the various tribes among the children of Israel.

Andrew Carnegie, a Scottish-American Industrialist, said that "no person will do a great business who wants to do it all himself or get all the credit." He once told a friend who told him that he got to work at seven in the morning: "You must be a lazy man if it takes you ten hours to do a day's work. What I do is get good men, and I never give them orders. My directions do not go beyond suggestions. Here in the morning, I get reports from them. Within an hour, I have disposed of everything, sent out all my suggestions, the day's work done, and I am ready to go out and enjoy myself." Rumsfeld served as the 13th Secretary of Defense from 1975 to 1977 under President Gerald Ford and the 21st Secretary of Defense from 2001 to 2006 under President George W. Bush. He is both the youngest and oldest person to have served as Secretary of Defense. "Don't be a bottleneck. If a matter is not a decision for the President or you, delegate it. Force responsibility down and out. Find problem areas, add structure, and delegate. The pressure is to do the reverse. Resist it."

Another leader who believes in delegating authority is David Ogilvy, widely hailed as "The Father of Advertising." Ogilvy's success can be tied directly back to his ability to hire smart people, delegate, and let them do their jobs. "Hire people who are better than you are, then leave them to get on with it. Look for people who will aim for the remarkable, who will not settle for the routine." According to Richard Branson, it's the simple ability of leaders to "delegate and let go." Mr. Branson also said, "If you really want to grow as an entrepreneur, you've got to learn to delegate."

In writing this book, I went through the daunting task of reviewing several pieces of literature on leadership and self-leadership. The literature reviewed consists of four primary focus areas: a) Core leadership theory, b) self-leadership concept, c) team-building intervention, and d) constructs of the study. In the area dedicated to core leadership theory, the reader will find a comprehensive review of core leadership theory and a review of past and current studies. The reader will find an exhaustive review of the professional and academic literature pertained to the great man theory, trait theory, behavioral theory, contingency theory, and influence theory. The self-leadership concept will be information on literature related to self-discovery, self-acceptance, self-management, and self-growth. According to Rambe, Modise, and Chipunza (2018), self-leadership and control are significant independent variables. When considered jointly, they have a significant positive impact on the job performance of the workforce. Additionally, a review of team-building intervention to include appropriate team-building activities, communication, and teamwork appeared in this study (Miller, Kim, Silverman, & Bauer, 2018).

This book discusses independent and dependent constructs, including authenticity, credibility, trust, and teamwork. According to Rosser, Grey, Neal, Reeve, Smith, and Valentine (2017), the outcomes of the cooperative inquiry include an enhanced understanding of the importance of openness and trust and a willingness to share and learn from each other in a respectful and confidential environment with a receptiveness to change. Rosser et al. (2018) determined that self-leadership is acceptable and embraced. Their collaboration has improved communication across the organization, enhanced their strategic leadership capability, and given self-assurance to disseminate externally. This statement means that the concept of self-leadership should be part of the organizational leadership development strategy.

Additionally, the literature review of this book includes a brief synopsis of some of the challenges that organizations are currently facing. Characteristics of those who identify as "Super-bosses" (Finkelstein, 2016). A pattern of corporate behavior churning through seasons of honesty, efficiency, deception, and redemption (Partridge, 2015). The process of leading organizational transformation (Gordon & Smith, 2015). The literature related to the concept of developing leaders to retain followers, the relationship between leaders and followers, and its impact on organizational success and employees' perception of their own leader's identity are reviewed as well. Only when leaders stop focusing on their ego needs can they become fully authentic and develop other leaders. Building trust and influence are the critical components of a leader (Glaser, 2014).

Leadership centers on vision, passion, direction, and most importantly, inspiring people to convey trust and contribute to the team's goal. Those who pride themselves as "super bosses" have these traits: they are all extremely competitive; they are visionaries; they manifest integrity: and strict adherence to a core vision or sense of self; and they are authentic (Finkelstein, 2016). A leader should be capable of inspiring team members to do tasks without micro-managing them. The author of "Super Bosses" (Finkelstein, 2016) posed the following questions to leaders: Do you have a specific vision for your work that energizes you and that you use to energize and inspire your team? How much affection or connection do members of your team feel with one another? What is the balance of competition and collaboration on the team? Do you continue to stay in touch with employees who have left to work elsewhere? Most books and articles on leadership do not have a concise list of attributes or traits that make for a great and successful leader.

This research focused on examining a new approach to aligning workers with an organization's mission, strategy, and goals (Irwin, 2018). You can find in some books less while others might have more characteristics but no standardized core drivers or attributes of successful leadership. However, this research tends to resolve that issue by exploring successful leaders' core leadership drivers and traits—the characteristics of those who identify as "super bosses" (Finkelstein, 2016). A pattern of corporate behavior churning through seasons of honesty, efficiency, deception, and redemption (Partridge, 2015). The process of leading organizational transformation. (Gordon, & Smith, 2015) Examples of how to add value to others as a leader. (Clark, 2015). Example of how a large organization can pivot quickly to accomplish a problematic mission (McChrystal, Collins, Silverman, & Fussell, 2015). Examples of the concept of applying science to create better teams (Karlgaard & Malone, 2015). Exploration of various perspectives in the creation of great leaders (Dempsey & Brafman, 2018). Examination of how talent can build trust and influence, two critical components of a leader (Glaser, 2014). Analysis of a new approach aligning workers with an organization's mission, strategy, and goals (Irwin, 2018). Key ideas and practices of servant leadership (Jennings & Stahl-Wert, 2016).

In researching the contents of this book, there were discrepancies in some pieces of literature reviewed. For instance, there were not many articles on leaders' lacking the skills they need to be effective today. Of the "top five" needs (inspiring commitment, strategic planning, leading people, resourcefulness, and employee development), only resourcefulness is considered a "top ten" skill (Leslie, 2009). Also, vision is a core concept that drives a leader's success versus motive, and there has been minimal discussion on the merging of leadership and followership. Leadership is a complex process where self-motivated relationships between leaders and followers in context are well thought-out. This research recommends a way forward in conceptualizing the attributes that make up the TEAM LEAD model as a function that drives the result for effective leadership, which reflects on overall job performance, leading to the leader's creation and retention of followers.

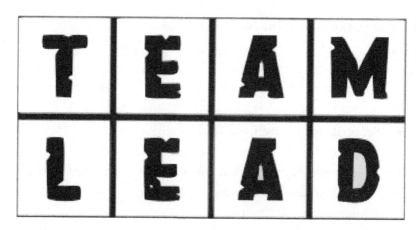

Leaders should encourage and motivate their followers as Apostle Paul did for Timothy in the Bible reference. Paul mentored Timothy to keep up the good work and not fail in his duty as a Christian. He urged him to follow the example he (Paul) showed him in dealing with other Christians and not emulate those who have decided not to model Christ as the Bible instructed them to do.

The Team Lead Model of Self-Leadership

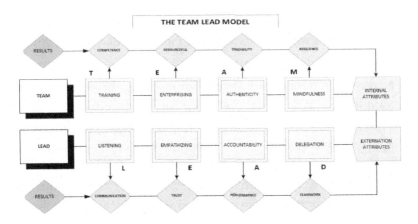

Figure 2: TEAM LEAD Model - Process flow

How To Develop These Skills Identified In The Framework Of The TEAM LEAD Model:

The first part of the acronym is T.E.A.M.

Training – this is a critical factor in the TEAM LEAD Model framework. How then do you develop new skills and become trained? Here are a few proven tips that will help you become competent as a leader:

- Set goals for yourself and find a mentor.
- Seek feedback about strengths and weaknesses.
- Take continuing education courses in career-related fields.
- Take advantage of organization training.
- Participate in job shadowing.

Enterprising – The enterprising mindset is another success factor identified in the TEAM LEAD Model framework. To develop an enterprising mindset, you must do the following:

- Be confident – seek and seize available opportunities.
- Be creative – apply critical thinking, and ask what if?
- Be flexible – be flexible with your thoughts and actions.

- Take calculated risks – anticipate potential mistakes but condition your mind to know that setbacks and mistakes are all part of a journey to success.
- Have self-belief – do not doubt yourself as not capable of achieving the goal.

Authenticity – This is yet another critical success factor identified in the TEAM LEAD Model framework. To become an authentic leader, you must do the following:

- Practice self-awareness and learn to tune into yourself.
- Learn and understand your strengths.
- Develop your emotional intelligence.
- Regular self-reflection.
- Focus on your values.

Mindfulness – To be mindful is yet another critical success factor identified in the TEAM LEAD Model that helps build resilience. The easiest way to be mindful every day is to do the following:

- Pay attention to what you do every day.
- Approach situations with curiosity.
- Take deep breaths when stressed.
- Appreciate the present.
- Learn to meditate.

The second part of the acronym is L.E.A.D. Here are additional tips on how to hone those skills:

Listening – Having an active listening skill is another critical success factor identified in the TEAM LEAD Model framework. To become an active listener, you must do the following:

- Pay attention - by giving the speaker your undivided attention and acknowledging the message they are sending.
- Show that you're listening - by using your body language and gestures to show that you are engaged.

- Provide feedback – reflect on what the other person said to ascertain your understanding of the issue. Your feedback should focus on the facts at hand.
- Defer judgment- active listening demands an open mind. It is vital to learn to withhold judgment even when you have strong opinions about the topic.
- Respond appropriately - you gain nothing by offending the speaker. Be candid and open-minded in your response.

Empathizing – Showing empathy is another critical success factor identified in the TEAM LEAD Model framework. To develop empathy, you must do the following:

- Put yourself in someone's position at the moment - by walking in the shoes of others.
- Step out of your comfort zone – mix with other cultures and appreciate the cultural differences.
- Examine your biases - explore and identify your prejudices by taking implicit association tests or through other means of self-analysis.
- Cultivate a curiosity mindset - ask more questions. Probably a little obvious but being more inquisitive does open the door to the curiosity that leads to learning.
- Read widely on various topics - someone who is well-read has a greater understanding and knows a lot about many subjects.

Accountability – Being accountable is another critical success factor identified in the TEAM LEAD Model framework. To develop an accountability mindset, you must do the following:

- Know your role and position.
- Understand your responsibilities to the people.
- Be honest by setting pride aside in your dealings.
- Be ready to apologize when something goes wrong.
- Don't overcommit but always take responsibility as a leader.

Delegation – Delegation of authority is another critical success factor identified in the TEAM LEAD Model framework. To delegate tasks effectively, you must do the following:

- Select the right person for the job.
- Explain why you are delegating the task.
- Provide proper instructions and guidance.
- Provide resources, training, and mentorship.
- Review the work, provide feedback, and say thank you.

The Process of Building a Cohesive Team

The research conducted for this book establishes the influence of self-leadership in Team Building. For optimum performance, a sense of belonging, and personal satisfaction, a leader must build a cohesive team. These are essential criteria in creating an environment where employees desire to continue to work and excel. Also, team cohesion promotes employees' engagement and commitment. In the previous pages, we discussed the framework of the TEAM LEAD model and identified eight critical factors required for efficient self-leadership. We also discussed how to hone those skills and behaviors to build a cohesive team to be an effective leader.

This section will discuss how to build a cohesive team by applying those vital attributes leaders require to be effective. The first thing to do is to develop a Mission and the Strategic Framework by using an Enterprising mindset; this will help the leader be more **Resourceful**. A resourceful leader will know that selecting team members is vital to look for diversity, which is the strength of a team and a critical component. Diversify in terms of skill, thought, technical background, and experience. An essential role of a leader is to establish Trust and Credibility; this study shows that it is one of the ingredients needed in team building. People should be able to trust you before they can work with you. To build Credibility and Trust, the leader must first apply **Authenticity** and **Empathy**, the third letter in TEAM, and the second letter in the LEAD model of the framework. Hence, being authentic and empathetic will help the leader achieve this goal and create an environment where the team can participate and have mutual respect.

> *For optimum performance, a sense of belonging, and personal satisfaction, a leader must build a cohesive team based on trust.*

As explained in the previous paragraph, the next step is to begin assembling the team with diversity in mind. At this time, you trust the caliber of the chosen people, and they trust your leadership capacity. To achieve this goal, the leader must be open to **feedback** even if they are not constructive. In developing **Mindfulness**, the leader will become more **Resilient** to any obstacle that comes their way. By applying Pareto's 80-20 principles, with only 20 percent resilience efforts, the leader becomes 80 percent effective in team building. Apply **Listening actively** to what the people are saying and their expectations of you as the leader. This phase will also help the leader to **communicate** their expectations to the people effectively. The leader must make sure that the **communication is consistent** and clearly explain the objectives, and all messages must be designed to the benefit of the team.

The next phase is to **determine the team's strengths** by identifying individual strengths with diversity in mind; this is the time to **Delegate** individual team members with specific tasks based on their strengths. Knowing their capacity will enable the leader to mentor the individual and help develop their capacity and team engagement and promote **Teamwork**. To achieve this, the leader should conduct additional feedback sessions to assess the individual intellectual capital. Sometimes leaders assume that the person they have in a position is the best fit without verifying if they can get the job done. The feedback section will also allow the leader to see what other team members bring to the table. In this phase of the process, the leader must embrace **Accountability**; this will help with **team performance,** as this research shows. In a cohesive team, everyone is accountable for their responsibilities by adopting the organization's strategic goals, and everyone is held accountable for the decisions and goals established.

Accountability will help the team to focus on results through their **Performances**.

The leader must remember to **reward** exceptional performance and **recognize** and **appreciate** the team members when they perform their job effectively by **celebrating** their **successes**. This effort will motivate the team members to execute more effectively next time. The last phase in the process of Team Building is continuous **Training; this** will help everyone become **competent**. Having the required skill and experience will help the team members to be proficient in doing their job. Training effectively will enable the leader to have the capacity and the capability to build a more cohesive team that has mutual trust and respect for one another. Here's a quote by Ronald Regan, "The greatest leader is not necessarily the one who does the greatest things. He is the one that gets the people to do the greatest things." I love this quote, "If your actions inspire others to dream more, learn more, do more, and become more, you are a leader" by John Quincy Adams.

Measuring Effectiveness of These Eight Traits in the Team Lead Model:

The most common measurement of a leader's effectiveness is assessing group performance and the scope to which the goals and objectives of the group are met. The degree to which this can be measured is a strong indicator that leaders can influence their subordinates and lead them to achieve the organization's strategic objectives. The leader should be able to answer the following questions:

Measuring a leader's competency as a result of the training:

- To what degree does the leader have an established succession plan -you know you're being effective when your employees shine and you feel confident enough to be hands-off to allow them to maximize their potential.

- To what degree are the strategic objectives being met against the growth metrics – the leader must align their personal goal to the organization's overall strategic goals.

- To what degree do the employees have a vote of confidence in the leader – The employee should trust that the leader can lead them in the right direction.
- To what degree does the workforce feel inspired by the decisions of the leader - When the team members understand the vision and can explain "why" the organization exists in the first place and their focus is more on service.

Measuring a leader's resourcefulness:
- To what degree is the leader able to adapt to a fast-changing environment.
- To what degree can the leader come up with creative ways to execute projects.
- To what degree can the leader find solutions with a minimal number of resources.
- To what degree can the leader take initiative and apply critical thinking in problem-solving

Measuring a leader's authenticity:
- To what degree is the leader aware of their strengths, limitations, and how others see the impact of their decisions (self-awareness).
- To what degree does the leader reinforce a level of openness with others that provides them with an opportunity to be forthcoming with their ideas, opinion, and challenges (transparency).
- To what degree does the leader set high moral standards and ethical conduct for themselves - Moral values pave the path for all their decisions in life.
- To what degree does the leader solicit enough opinion and viewpoints before making important decisions that will affect a larger number of people.

Measuring a leader's resilience:

- To what degree can the leader handle complaints from the workforce – a resilient leader is not intimidated by attacks or complaints that seem personal.

- To what degree can the leader accept feedback that is not constructive from the workforce – negative feedback, process it thoughtfully, and respond by making necessary changes.

- To what degree does the leader exhibit curiosity and open-mindedness - Curiosity enables the leader to shift perspective, not judgmental, to explore greater possibilities.

- To what degree can the leader work under pressure with competing priorities – Performing well under pressure is both a personal and professional quality that makes a leader effective.

Measuring a leader's effective communication:

- Targeted communication - To what degree can the leader determine the current state of communication or the communication battle rhythm.

- To what degree does the leader know who the targeted audience should be reached and how to reach them.

- To what degree can the leader frame a message that resonates with your target audience - how well can the leaders connect with the right audience.

- To what degree can the leader track who and when the message is received and if the audience can identify the benefit of the message to them.

Measuring the leader's trustworthiness:

- To what degree does the leader demonstrate competence in their given role or function and does their track record show success and give employees confidence in their abilities.

- To what degree is the leader believable while showing integrity - A believable leader is honest, credible, authentic, and takes responsibility for their mistakes and actions.

- To what degree can the leader connect with the workforce – a leader that can connect with the followers immediately demonstrates trustworthiness by leveling with the followers.

- To what degree is the leader dependable – Can the followers rely on the leader to commit to what he or she said they will do to build trust with the followers.

Measuring a leader's accountability:

- To what degree can the leader take personal responsibility - Personal responsibility is the willingness to view yourself as the principal source of results and circumstances that occur in your life.

- To what degree is the leader personally empowered to perform effectively – Personal empowerment is an internally-derived capacity to perform at or above an established level of expectation.

- To what degree can the leader measure the employees' understanding of how their work contributes to organizational goals and priorities.

- To what degree does the leader know that employees have the needed resources to accomplish the task to ensure they meet their goals.

Measuring a leader's ability to delegate work:

- To what degree does the leader understand when, how, and who to delegate tasks - does the task provide an opportunity to grow and develop another person's skills.

- To what degree can the leader match the amount of responsibility with the authority – the leader can delegate responsibility but be accountable for the outcome.

- To what degree can the leader identify constraints and boundaries – the leader should know the lines of authority, responsibility, and accountability.

- To what degree can the leader tolerate risks and mistakes, and use them as learning opportunities, rather than an excuse not to delegate in the first place.

The practical way to measure a leader's effectiveness (e.g., to measure effectiveness in Accountability follow these steps)

	Low - 1	Moderate - 3	High - 5	Count
To what degree can the leader take personal responsibility.	X			1
To what degree is the leader personally empowered to perform effectively.		X		3
To what degree can the leader measure the employees' understanding of how their work contributes to organizational goals and priorities.			X	5
To what degree does the leader know that employees have the needed resources to accomplish the task to ensure they meet their goals.		X		3
Total Count	1	6	5	12
1-4 = Ineffective 5-8 = Near Success 9-12 = Effectiveness				

CHAPTER 5

RELATIONSHIP BETWEEN CONSTRUCTS

Learning Objectives:

- Understand the relationship between the constructs

- Understand the leadership challenge

- Familiarity with the rationale for this research

- The conceptual framework for self-leadership

- Understand specific self-leadership attributes

The TEAM LEAD concept explained in this book is imperative to individuals and organizations who desire to improve their leadership skills by applying the TEAM LEAD Model of self-leadership. To achieve the purpose of this book, and test the fidelity of the TEAM LEAD model, we explored the influence of self-leadership on team-building abilities among leaders within an unidentified U.S. Government agency. This book addressed the lack of self-leadership among leaders resulting in ineffective team building. This book will assist leaders in discovering that the TEAM LEAD model is a tool, approach, skill, methodology, or theory needed to prepare those in authority for self-leadership better to assist team building and evaluate this tool, method, or theory. To support this paradigm, specific questions were asked during this research to explore how self-leadership influences team-building abilities among leaders. Also, we will discuss barriers to self-leadership that prevent team building among leaders.

This book addresses the concept of self-leadership and the relationship of attributes such as authenticity, credibility, and trust to the team-building abilities among leaders. Twenty leaders were interviewed using convenience sampling to understand self-leadership and how that relates to team building that results in teamwork. In the analysis of the interview data, seven shared themes were identified. The themes developed from the study are relevant and applicable in today's business environment due to the value and the positive impact of self-leadership in team building, resulting in enhanced leadership competence and success in organizations. There were recommendations for action developed to support the declaration that organizational leaders and businesses establish the TEAM LEAD Model self-leadership training curriculum in their leadership development programs. This book properly explains the rationale for the TEAM LEAD framework by exploring self-leadership influence in team building.

The primary purpose of conducting my research and writing this book is to inform action and show how the TEAM LEAD theory contributes to the leadership discourse, adding to the body of knowledge in the self-leadership field of study. The influence of self-leadership studies traces its origin in the Western ecclesial perspectives on leadership (Lynch, 2019). This research, in particular, fulfilled the requirement by interviewing identified participants that have first-hand information on the role that self-leadership plays in team building and the influence of self-leadership on the employees' decisions in team activities. This qualitative case study contributes to the literature in significant ways, such as exploring the association between self-leadership and team building, drawing on team leadership theory, and recommending attributes that influence self-leadership (Lynch, 2019).

The study conducted by Land (2019) emphasized that team building can have lasting, positive, and measurable effects on team performance and that managers should account for team-building activities in their planning. Land (2019) highlighted that giving a team the chance to spend time together to participate in some fun activity together may not make them into a better performing team long-term. Another study conducted by Lee and Paunova (2017) determined that organizational leadership continually recognizes a self-managed team through self-leadership. The study results are of great benefit to organizational leadership. Data collected will provide the leaders with information on how self-leadership can help improve team-building abilities. The results of this research will enable leaders to improve leadership skills in the area of team building. This study will foster new ways of enhancing knowledge, skills, and attitude, thus preparing globally competitive leaders in the future.

This book will be of great benefit to every leader and aspiring leader. Data collected provide leaders with information on how self-leadership can help improve team-building abilities. The results will enable the leaders to enhance leadership skills in the area of team building. Data gathered highlights the importance of self-leadership in enhancing authenticity, credibility, and trust in leaders, resulting in eliminating challenges that hinder team building (Mayiams & Raffo, 2018). This study will improve any organization in the development of self-leadership training. This study will foster new ways of enhancing knowledge, skills, and attitude, thus preparing globally competitive leaders in the future (Mayiams & Raffo, 2018). This study will also help in the advancement of the leadership development program and self-leadership skills.

This study analyzes a government agency's leadership development program, the leader's approach, self-leadership skills learned, the quality of training rendered, and team-building abilities. This research is related to the field of study, which is leadership. Zigarmi (2018) views leadership as a process of influence and is most often referenced in relation to serving, motivating, and empowering others. Zigarmi (2018) emphasized that self-leadership is about developing and managing your energy to initiate, encourage, perform at a high level, improve, and sustain your organization's leadership philosophy at an individual level. According to Lynch (2019), managerialism is a particular cultural narrative that has influenced leadership studies' broader field.

This book highlights the significance of the relational leadership concept through the reduction of self-leadership gaps. This study addresses the gap in self-leadership that, if decreased, will enhance authenticity, credibility, and trust resulting in team building among leaders. This study provided information regarding the importance of self-leadership in the context of the leader's team-building ability, which will help leaders improve individual and organizational performance (Browning, 2018). This study will help develop a sense of self-leadership and the leader's ability to influence communication, emotions, and behaviors (Browning, 2018). This study addresses the challenges that hinder self-leadership, resulting in the agency's failure to retain talented leaders with team-building abilities. This study highlighted and reduced the gap between self-leadership and a leader's team-building ability of some leaders in the federal government by applying the TEAM LEAD model of self-leadership explained in this book.

The rationale for undertaking this research. To explore self-leadership influence in team building by using the eight-core attributes in the TEAM LEAD model for effective leadership in an organization. This book addresses the relationship between self-leadership and attributes such as authenticity, credibility, and trust in team-building abilities among leaders. Stewart, Courtright, and Manz (2019) argued that self-leadership progressed from focusing on individual self-influence processes to understanding self-influence processes at the team level. According to Stewart et al. (2019), self-leadership reflects a higher degree of control where individuals apply self-management strategies, assess the relevance of existing standards, and set their standards. Hunt, Heilman, Shutran, and Wu (2017) asserted that effective leadership is associated with self-awareness. Hunt et al. (2017) suggested that encouraging organization-supported, self-initiated leadership development behaviors are imperative in leadership development strategy.

Bendell, Sullivan, and Marvel (2019) suggested that self-leadership specifies a collection of intra-individual strategies that provide explicit behavioral and cognitive prescriptions to achieve greater personal effectiveness. Rosser, Grey, Neal, Reeve, Smith, and Valentine (2017) emphasized that scholars have embraced self-leadership and that self-leadership collaboration has improved communication across organizations and enhanced strategic leadership capability. Browning

(2018) asserts that self-leadership helps leaders build stronger relationships, and become more self-aware and disciplined. According to Knutson (2020), self-leadership practitioners should consider two types of self-leadership: behavioral self-leadership and mental self-leadership. Knutson (2020) suggested that behavioral self-leadership deals with goal setting, monitoring behavior, and evaluating progress, while mental self-leadership can alter a leader's self-dialogue, beliefs, and thought patterns.

The Leadership Challenge. This study primarily focuses on the lack of understanding of the self-leadership training concept and explores the influence of self-leadership in team-building efforts. Stewart, Courtright, and Manz (2019) suggested that leaders could make the team chartering a focus of team development efforts because developing charters appears to help reduce process losses. Team members that need team charters the most are probably the least likely to engage in team charter exercises. Self-leadership training often involves making choices that allow a person to navigate challenges and opportunities to perform at a higher level. Khan and Wajidi (2019) emphasized that in organizational development, team building functions are central not only for the immediate experience of the team's activities but the group expertise, communication, and bonding. Khan and Wajidi (2019) agreed that effective leadership and team-building might eliminate the dilemmas and problems in organizations at times.

Browning (2018) grasps a deeper understanding of the importance and relevance of core leadership theories. Leaders who practice self-leadership are more fully aware of the inconsistencies in their lives and prefer to look inward. Leaders tend to focus on external factors rather than internal factors when solving organizational problems. According to Bryant (2021), self-leadership is the answer to an individual's development, survival, and thriving in a volatile, complex, and uncertain world. Bryant (2021) advised that self-leadership is the solution for developing leaders and leadership teams to communicate and apply creativity with critical thinking and collaboration. Fung (2018) questioned whether leadership roles could significantly influence team building and participation. Leadership roles indirectly influence team shared mental models via team building participation and shared knowledge on team members' characteristics and showing team interaction patterns.

Self-leadership enhances a leader's ability to manage intrapersonal and interpersonal relationships and skills that involve leaders' abilities to reflect on self-strengths and weaknesses (Browning, 2018). Serving as a leader who can build team cohesiveness is the best commitment embarked upon by individuals (Matsumura & Ogawa, 2017). Successful organizations focus on team development in their daily activities (Dyer & Dyer, 2020). Teams should feel good about working together and developing themselves (Chatham-Newstex, 2017). There is a greater need for individuals with technical expertise to create sustainable, workable solutions to serve in leadership positions (Knight, & Novoselich, 2017). Another focus of self-leadership practice is relational coordination, which is essential for leadership development professionals to empower teams to reach higher problem-solving levels (Jones-Schenk, 2018).

The general focus of this research is the lack of self-leadership among organizations' leaders, resulting in ineffective team building. The lack of self-development, and the need to understand oneself, causes a leader's lack of self-efficacy when addressing population needs (DeWitt, 2018). Inefficient leadership is prevalent in various organizations (Matsumura & Ogawa, 2017). Ineffective leadership can seriously affect employee morale and even cause the organization's bottom line to plunge. Incompetent leaders will result in low employee retention and demoralization, causing the employees to be much less productive as a team. Ineffective leadership at the professional level impedes the dissemination of policies beneficial for organizational success (Crabtree, Howard, Miller, Cromp, Hsu, Coleman., Austin, Flinter, Tuzzio, & Wagner, 2020). The inability of leadership to respond to ongoing policy demands will result in moral distress and burnout (Crabtree et al., 2020).

According to Blanchard (2017), organizational initiatives fail because the people responsible for the implementation do not have the leadership skills required for success. The lack of supportive leaders could considerably strain employees' health and job performance

(Schmidt, Herr, Jarczok, Baumert, Lukaschek, Emeny, & Ladwig, 2018). The leader's inefficiency becomes detrimental to the employees as a result of the stress. The workforce's health is an essential issue in public health research, gaining increased attention in recent years (Schmidt et al., 2018).

The specific problem addressed in this book was the lack of self-leadership in an organization resulting in ineffective team-building ability. A private leadership strategy is more improved than public leadership strategy from a social welfare perspective if the private firm is local, regardless of differentiation (Matsumura & Ogawa, 2017). This research accounts for self-leadership training opportunities for the frontline employees to grow and develop to their full potential to support team-building interventions among leaders. Another focus of this study is to explore explanatory factors such as communication, teamwork, and core leadership theories that help an individual self-leadership. Crabtree et al. (2020) suggest that current and future leaders' training should be comprehensive, motivating, and focused on developing effective teams.

Another problem is that senior management's weak leadership affects the quality of performance at the program level (Parvin, 2019). There is a lack of an efficient leadership development program because management continuously focuses on routine administrative work (Parvin, 2019). This regular administrative work is devoid of leaders' basic management tasks, such as gathering and utilizing information, planning strategically, effectively managing, and developing employees (Parvin, 2019). Leaders should apply the strategy of team-building intervention and focus on the outcomes of the team-building activities. The reason is that there is an increasing organizational focus on a team-based format that emphasizes interdisciplinary coordination (Miller, Kim, Silverman, & Bauer, 2018). A study suggests that leadership training evaluations for team-building interventions were generally positive (Miller et al., 2018).

The nature of the study. A qualitative research method and a multiple case study apply to this research (Collins & Stockton, 2018). It is the appropriate methodology for this study because this qualitative approach addresses the problem statement: self-leadership, enhancing authenticity, credibility, and trust that support team building among leaders. The qualitative research method is more likely to produce high-impact findings (Jamali, 2018). According to Marx (2017), high-quality qualitative research is interpretive. This research's data collection method involves interviewing participants to help understand and explore the participant's experiences. Jamali (2018) posits that the qualitative method will help evaluate interviewees' answers with a unique perspective, prompting additional discussions during the questioning process.

Open-ended questions helped to discover information that individuals might overlook. Individual participation is critical to the success of this research. Goldsby, Goldsby, and Neck (2020) assert that self-leadership cognitive strategies place responsibility for an individual's thought patterns. Discussion of the reason for not selecting other methods: the reason for not choosing other methods is due to the vital strength of qualitative research methods, in particular, being able to collate relevant contextual data alongside quantitative preference data (Vass, Rigby, & Payne, 2017). This assertion means collecting pertinent data for research is beneficial if studies are appropriate and reported with sufficient clarity. Readers can understand the approach used and interpret the findings (Vass, Rigby, & Payne, 2017).

The qualitative research method applies qualitative approaches to collect data, analyze, interpret, and write the report, which differs from the traditional quantitative approaches (Creswell & Creswell, 2017). The qualitative research method supports purposeful sampling, collection of open-ended data, and analysis of text or images, diagrams, and pictures. Other representations of information in figures and tables and personal interpretations of the findings inform qualitative methods (Creswell & Creswell, 2017). The reason for choosing the qualitative case study design is for better exploratory research and to help generate new ideas. A qualitative case study is also distinct and provides value to the audience (Waldner, Cyr, Koivu, & Goertz, 2019). A qualitative case study will provide the tools to examine complex situations and create excellent outcomes from the analysis; this research will help with an in-depth analysis of self-leadership to discover common interventions and strategies for working with leaders and building stronger teams.

Additionally, the qualitative portion of a multimethod research design represents little more than a triangulation check on the theoretical insights gleaned from quantitative analysis (Waldner, Cyr, Koivu, & Goertz, 2019). Also, regarding data collection, interview and survey methods are the best choices in this qualitative research method, including online surveys and one-on-one consultations over the phone due to the current global COVID-19 pandemic. Another data collection method is to distribute surveys to diverse candidates and request their completion within a period, and follow-up interviews will help gather additional data for the research (Harper & McCunn, 2017).

As a result of the global COVID-19 pandemic, there is no need to assemble a focus group in a room. A video conference is an option if the focus group will help because of these pandemic restrictions. Participation in this qualitative research is voluntary, and this results in limited candidates' availability. Some may have a change of mind and not participate in the interview or answer the survey questionnaire due to unforeseen circumstances. However, backup candidates will be available when this occurs. Utilizing the observation/participant observation method could prove challenging at times (Harper & McCunn, 2017). The goal is to identify gaps in self-leadership by using open-ended questions in this qualitative case study (Harper & McCunn, 2017). Another data collection method will combine surveys with qualitative research interviews (Öhman, Keisu, & Enberg, 2017). The above claim means that the study can measure self-leadership and specific team-building abilities among leaders in organizations. This case study will focus on self-leadership attributes in open-ended questions and free-listing questions about self-leadership (Öhman, Keisu, & Enberg, 2017).

The interview guide could elaborate on the major themes from the open-ended questions that will focus on variables such as the importance of the work team, leadership, career development opportunities, rewards, influence, and decision-making analysis. The survey could constitute a point of departure for the qualitative interviews

(Öhman, Keisu, & Enberg, 2017). The reason for selecting a multiple case study design and no other designs is because the multiple case study design can predict contrasting results for common reasons (Gustafsson, 2018). Other advantages of multiple-case studies are that they create a more convincing theory when the suggestions are more grounded in several empirical pieces of evidence (Gustafsson, 2018).

A multiple case study is a design of inquiry found in many fields, especially in the evaluation of developing an in-depth analysis of a case, often a program, event, activity, process, and one or more individuals (Creswell & Creswell, 2017). Time and activity can restrict multiple case studies due to efforts to collect detailed information using various data collection procedures over a sustained period (Creswell & Creswell, 2017). Mixed methods design involves combining qualitative and quantitative research and data in a research study (Creswell & Creswell, 2017). A case study investigates a contemporary phenomenon in a real-life situation when the boundaries between the object of research and context are not evident (Ebneyamini & Sadeghi Moghadam, 2018). Using a multiple-case design is a more extensive exploration of the research question, and theoretical evolution will enable an individual to understand the differences and similarities of information management (Brink, 2018).

Triangulation is crucial in this multiple case study research, especially in triangulating data sources or methods (Gustafsson, 2018). Triangulation supports a more accurate, comprehensive, and objective representation of the data (Gustafsson, 2018). A case study copes with the technically distinctive situation in which there may be many more variables of interest than data points. One result relies on multiple sources of evidence, with data needing coverage in a triangulating fashion (Ebneyamini & Sadeghi Moghadam, 2018). A case study captures the complexity of a single case, and the methodology that enables this has developed within the social sciences (Ebneyamini & Sadeghi Moghadam, 2018). A qualitative case study methodology is also applicable in the social sciences, such as psychology, sociology, anthropology, and economics (Ebneyamini & Sadeghi Moghadam, 2018).

The qualitative case study methodology allows researchers to study complex cases within a set framework (Ebneyamini & Sadeghi Moghadam, 2018). A case study is one of the most flexible qualitative research approaches (Collins & Stockton, 2018). Applying the multiple case study approach could result in a valuable method of developing the self-leadership theory, evaluating programs, and developing interventions (Ebneyamini & Sadeghi Moghadam, 2018).

Multiple current perspectives from research methodologists: to increase the traceability and credibility of qualitative research, and secondly, to help make the complexity of Multiple Perspectives Qualitative Longitudinal Interviews (MPQLI) manageable (Vogl, Zartler, Schmidt, & Rieder, 2018). Addressing this methodological gap, we first briefly introduce the potential of qualitative longitudinal research and multiple perspective interviews (Vogl et al., 2018). The authors combined these two approaches to develop an analytical framework for MPQLI and illustrated the suggested procedure with empirical examples (Vogl et al., 2018). They can take the form of interviews with respondents of similar characteristics (e.g., mothers) and interviews with different types of respondents (Vogl et al., 2018).

From a different perspective, qualitative analysis of the interviews proceeded in several methodological steps. In line with the qualitative paradigm, it defines breadwinning very broadly and de-gendered as specific meaning parents attach to the money earned; for instance, the opportunity to provide for the family and focusing on how both parents within one couple construct this meaning (Schmidt, 2018). Another study suggested that further research should address these methodological challenges of analyzing multiple perspective qualitative data. Specifically, for deeper saturation, research should further include more contrasting cases (Schmidt, 2018). There are benefits to applying in-depth interpretive analysis of multiple-perspective and qualitative interviews because of the opportunity to get varieties of perspectives unexploited in the process (Schmidt, 2018). Qualitative data analysis inspires the constant comparative method in grounded theory, which is not applicable in this research framework (Larsson & Björk, 2017).

Discussion of the research method for this book - this qualitative research focuses on the qualitative case study method. Qualitative research refers to a broad range of philosophies, approaches, and methods used to acquire an in-depth understanding or explanation of people's perceptions (Vass, Rigby, & Payne, 2017). Qualitative case study methods explore peoples' thoughts or feelings by collecting verbal or textual data (Vass et al., 2017). Evolving research methodology creates opportunities for investigators to understand the topic (Kharasch, 2019). This methodology will help non-experts understand this research and obtain data to translate self-leadership knowledge (Kharasch, 2019). Qualitative case study research aims to understand the phenomena in context-specific settings, such as a real-world setting (Brink,2018).

The reason for selecting a qualitative case study is to understand better how self-leadership influences team building (Brink,2018). Study shows that qualitative research has grown in popularity towards facilitating the authentic expression of the complex realities of people engaged through research (Woodgate, Zurba, & Tennent, 2017). In this qualitative case study, interviews as a data collection method help give an extensive response to the research question (Brink, 2018). The data collected from either the interview or the survey may differ in the quality and quantity of the research conducted (Brink, 2018). On the other hand, the data coming through qualitative research can generate meaningful changes to the organization by informing policy-makers (Woodgate, Zurba, & Tennent, 2017). Other data collection methods such as surveys, observations, focus groups, and experiments are not optimal or suited for this current study.

Discussion of design of the research of this book - the qualitative research design consists of five distinctive designs: the narrative research design, the phenomenology research design, grounded theory research design, ethnography research design, and the case study research design (Creswell & Creswell, 2017). This research will focus on the qualitative case study method (Gustafsson, 2018). The qualitative case study method will explore the influence of self-leadership on team-building abilities (Gustafsson, 2018). The coverage of research designs limits the frequently used forms such as surveys and experiments in quantitative research, narrative research, phenomenology, grounded theory, ethnography, and case studies in qualitative research (Creswell & Creswell, 2017). Additionally, the design used is the qualitative research design which is crucial for any educational study to enable a deeper understanding of experiences, phenomena, and context (Harris, 2020).

Qualitative research design ensures that the data obtained help answer the research question (Bakker, 2019). The reason to conduct research is to learn by getting answers from all data collected. According to Bakker (2019), research design claims to have the potential to bridge the gap between educational practice and theory because research design helps to develop theories about domain-specific learning. Harris (2020) declared that one of the severe difficulties with research design, especially with reviewing literature in research design, is how much to learn. This qualitative case study illustrates the self-leadership influence on the team-building experience of the participants. Mixed methods designs are not the optimal choice for this study because of the difficulty in comparing two analyses using different mixed methods designs. In contrast, quantitative design collects a much narrower and sometimes superficial dataset and is unsuitable for this study.

The data collection method, such as interviews and surveys, will help the target audience and peer research, ensure that the results from this qualitative research are obtained in a logical and unbiased way, and show the number of participants in this research (Prominski & Seggern, 2019). This qualitative research allows learning, data creation, and data collection used for this qualitative case study (Prominski & Seggern, 2019). This research method and design highlights this qualitative research's significant structures and traits through the data collection method such as interviews and surveys (Johnson, Tod, Brummell, & Collins, 2018). Unlike other research designs, the case study design is more appropriate to provide more insight into this research (Gustafsson, 2018).

The researcher relies on qualitative research design and method to conclude the importance of the self-leadership concept in team-building and explore previous literature on the research topic (Johnson et al.,

2018). This research design ensures minimum bias in data and increases trust in data collected for accuracy. Although not in this case, in common with other qualitative studies, potential observer bias and the risk of post hoc justification among interviewees can influence the results (Johnson et al., 2018). The ethics of research methodology and methodology of research ethics can develop in productive interaction (Knottnerus & Tugwell, 2018).

To support the analysis of this research, the research questions needed to form the basis of examining the role of leadership in addressing self-leadership in an organization. This specific research question helps the researcher make decisions about study design and population and subsequently through data collected and analyzed (Lane, 2018). A good research question forms the backbone of good research, which is vital in unraveling nature's mysteries and giving insight into a problem (Ratan, Anand, & Ratan, 2019). Research questions must be academically and intellectually engaging to people in the field the researcher has chosen to study (Ratan, Anand, & Ratan, 2019). This research seeks to answer the following questions: how does self-leadership support team-building abilities among leaders in an organization? What barriers, if any, to self-leadership could prevent team building among leaders in an organization?

These research questions are related to the problem statement because the questions highlight the importance of self-leadership in team-building abilities among leaders in an organization. Self-leadership could be as simple as a self-goal setting. According to Müller and Niessen (2019), a self-goal setting is necessary when employees are responsible for their work outcomes. Employees can determine the working rhythm rather than be externally regulated by a particular leader in the organization. According to Lane (2018), if a research question is well-posed in the study's design, the participant's ability to answer the question will often fall easily into place. Lane (2018) emphasized that ideally, the research question should determine the best design for the study and that a good research question often starts with a general observation.

The research conducted for this book explored the concepts of self-leadership in an organization that enhances authenticity, credibility, and trust, supporting team-building among leaders. Maximo, Stander, and Coxen (2019) stated that leaders could develop collaborative relationships, and build credibility and respect from subordinates when they act authentically. Maximo, Stander, and Coxen (2019) determined that authentic leadership is not only a significant predictor of work engagement but that authenticity impacts work engagement indirectly by trusting the leader. There will be a discussion on the role of self-leadership in addressing team building in an organization. Another study conducted by Donahue (2018) stated that trust is a central variable in determining an organization's effectiveness and business performance. Donahue (2018) resolved that an authentic leader must build trust and win respect in the organization.

The concept of authenticity. The idea of being genuine and original. Parker (2017) stated that authenticity marks effective leaders, as trust is the basis of every relationship. Parker (2017) further emphasized that authenticity allows a leader to show imperfection and an element of humanity that generates trust. This notion means that an authentic leader's integrity is never in question. Hence, to be an authentic leader, you start by knowing yourself, which is self-awareness. Steckler and Clark (2019) suggested that authenticity provides a valuable lens to consider how leaders can bring a firm's strategy and practices into better alignment with the firm core values. Authenticity offers a much-needed lens for incorporating personal virtue into the theory. According to Guenter, Gardner, Davis McCauley, Randolph-Seng, and Prabhu (2017), leaders can distribute roles among team members. Guenter et al. (2017) suggest that change at varying points depends on which members meet the team's needs and are carried out authentically with the team's admirations.

The concept of credibility. Leadership credibility has a significant impact on public perception of that leader (Hearn, 2019). The lack of credibility could directly undermine policy promotion if viewed as untrustworthy (Hearn, 2019). Credibility focuses on leaders' role and their ability to coordinate followers' actions through credibility (Hearn,

2019). This claim means that a credible leader shows experience, skill, and trustworthiness and that leader's ability to influence individuals will help to build a cohesive team. According to Cooper, Hamman, and Weber (2020), a leader must have the ability to convince followers that the conditions are favorable. Cooper, Hamman, and Weber (2020) emphasized that a leader may gain in the short run by encouraging actions that do not benefit the followers but lose in the long run if these actions destroy his credibility.

The concept of trust. According to previous research findings by Javed, Rawwas, Khandai, Shahid, and Hafiz (2018), trust is essential in explaining the relationship between ethical leaders and creativity, and trust plays a vital role in the relationship between leaders and their employees, and effective trust shows positive consequence. Javed et al. (2018) noted that regardless of the significance, the literature on the effect of trust on creativity remains inconclusive. Without trust in leaders, employees may be hesitant to share ideas and communicate with the leader. According to Peragine and Hudgins (2017), trust is one of the significant factors that teammates should experience to be successful; the same analysis suggests that a team leader needs to build loyalty and choose individuals who can work together. Magpili-Smith (2017) advocates that the lack of team trust can inhibit the information elaboration process in teams because of the social-categorization process. Magpili-Smith (2017) determined that teams with long-term relationships usually form trust based on experiences.

The concept of teamwork. Teamwork is a familiar notion within several theoretical models. According to McEwan, Ruissen, Eys, Zumbo, and Beauchamp (2017), teamwork comprises multiple observable and measurable behaviors. The outcome is that organizations must align to support teamwork and collaboration, meaning that senior leadership signals that teamwork is essential. Leaders are the engine that fosters teamwork, and they set the culture for teamwork (Salas, Reyes, & McDaniel, 2018). Teamwork can enable team members to have a higher level of emotional security, self-confidence, and the ability to positively plan and decide with others (Sanyal & Hisam, 2018). Teamwork helps develop employees' skills and perspectives by exchanging positive opinions, feedback, experiences, and viewpoints (Sanyal & Hisam, 2018).

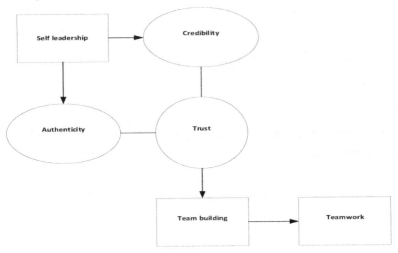

Figure 3. Relationship to constructs.

Relationships between attributes - a study conducted by Hoang, Liu, Pratt, Zheng, Chang, Roughead, and Li (2018) emphasizes a mutual interaction between authenticity and credibility. Such interaction enables changes in one factor to affect the prediction of the others. Maximo, Stander, and Coxen (2019) proposed that having more authentic leaders could enhance trust and that authentic leadership had a statistically significant indirect effect on work engagement through trust in leaders. Saffran, Hu, Hinnant, Scherer, and Nagel (2020) maintained that authenticity measures the context of communication that can shape trust and credibility. Saffran et al. (2020) emphasized that teamwork is the result of building a cohesive team.

The Conceptual Framework for Self-leadership

The research concepts explore the influence of self-leadership in an organization that enhances authenticity, credibility, and trust, supporting team-building among leaders. Team building is the required method of improving the emotional climate in which teams operate and overall team functioning (Beauchamp, McEwan, & Waldhauser, 2017). This conceptual framework illustrates this study's findings and how authenticity, credibility, and trust are related to developing self-leadership in team building. Ibus and Ismail (2018) resolved that a behavioral-focused strategy helps manage one's behavior, incorporating self-attention, self-observation, self-goal setting, self-reward, self-correcting, and feedback.

Guillotin and Mangematin (2018) emphasized that authenticity results in a leader's credibility. The authors further concluded that authenticity emphasizes the distinctive nature of the reader's experience. Leveraging that habit could allow leaders to differentiate themselves and maintain credibility among their followers. According to Parker (2017), individuals with honed self-awareness create a space for authenticity and growth. The author further stated that authenticity allows a leader to show imperfection and an element of humanity that generates trust in a team.

Self-Leadership Attributes

Authenticity. Authenticity is a critical aspect of leadership, and authentic leaders lead with integrity (Covelli & Mason, 2017). The authors further stated that authentic leadership is a multi-dimensional leadership theory. Therefore, it has similarities to transformational theory and several other leadership theories, including ethical, charismatic, spiritual, and servant leadership. According to Ling, Liu, and Wu (2017), authentic leadership influences employee work attitudes through a group trust climate. Coetzer, Bussin, and Geldenhuys (2017) describe authenticity as showing one's true identity, intentions, and motivations.

Credibility. Merriam-Webster dictionary (2020) defines credibility as the quality of believing an individual or being accepted as authentic, genuine, or honest. Mayiams, Raffo, and Clark (2018) determine credibility as an extension of trust. Mayiams, Raffo, and Clark (2018) further described credibility as the quality that enables one to be believed and involves the trustworthiness and reliability of information or communication received from a person. According to Fernandez and Shaw (2020), if the leader is not credible, the message communicated may not be credible. This assertion means that leaders should be trustworthy in what they say to their followers or the public.

Trust. Trust in the leader has a significantly positive influence on the followers' work engagement. Engelbrecht, Heine, and Mahembe (2017) support the notion that trust is built on ethical leaders' behaviors such as integrity and reliability, which likely results in trust that subordinates may reciprocate. The authors concluded that the degree to which the leader is trustworthy might influence how the followers place confidence, trust, and belief in the leader. The study conducted by Lesinger, Altinay, Altinay, and Dagli (2018) determined that trustworthiness is a critical concept that fosters trust through loyalty and leadership.

Assumptions - critically examining constructs in scholarly literature is vital for understanding fundamental assumptions about what counts in any research (Wolgemuth, Hicks, & Agosto, 2017). The findings produced by the research synthesis constitute these assumptions, and exploring excluded evidence reveals the implications of those decisions (Wolgemuth, Hicks, & Agosto, 2017).

The underlying assumption is that self-leadership will continue to be important in any organization. Another assumption is that participants will respond truthfully and are knowledgeable, although no verification of participants in this study. The participants will answer the interview questions honestly and truthfully. Therefore, the sample's inclusion criteria are appropriate, and they ensure that the participants have experienced the same or similar study phenomenon. Participants should have a sincere interest in participating in this research with no alternative motives. Although participants understand the significance of honest reporting, research suggests that some participants typically lie (Montgomery, Mensch, Musara, Hartmann, Woeber, Etima, & van der Straten, 2017).

Limitations. This study's limitations concern potential weaknesses outside this research's boundaries and are closely associated with the chosen research design, statistical model constraints, funding constraints, or other factors. Theofanidis and Fountouki (2018) defined limitation as an imposed restriction outside the control of any individual, while delimitation is anything within the control of an individual. Limitations also refer to potential weaknesses and sample size too small to generalize the study. A research method is a process for conducting this research, such as collecting data through interviews and surveys. The survey method produced relatively short answers that were straight to the point. The interview method gives extensive responses expected in qualitative research. To mitigate this is by asking participants who provide the data whether the interpretations represent their beliefs.

> *Delimitation defines the constraints or weaknesses, which are not within the control of the researcher, therefore, they are not expected to be covered in the study.*

There is no replication of this case study, and there is no generalization of the single case study to a broader population. Another limitation is that there is a potential risk for bias in case studies, in that an individual's beliefs can influence the data collection and analysis method. The attempt to mitigate bias is by asking peers to review the conclusions; they might identify and address any argument gaps. Another limitation is cultural bias because most organizational participants are not always honest when responding to the interview questionnaire (Montgomery, Mensch, Musara, Hartmann, Woeber, Etima, & van der Straten, 2017).

Delimitations. Delimitations refer to the boundaries selected in the population, and the scope is only some aspects of the study's leadership (Theofanidis & Fountouki, 2018). This study's limitation is that only those in leadership positions participated in the interview. There was no access to personal or sensitive data for this research and discussed in this research process. The study used only pseudo names, no real names of the participants, to maintain every participant's privacy. Delimitations are set so that the researcher's goals do not become large to complete. Examples of delimitations include the sample size, geographical location or setting in which the study will take place, population traits, objectives, research questions, variables, theoretical objectives that the researcher has adopted, and populations chosen as targets to study.

CHAPTER 6

SELF-LEADERSHIP PERCEPTION

Learning Objective:

- Understand the concept of self-assessment

- Understand the concept of self-acceptance

- Understand the concept of self-discovery

- Understand the concept of self-management

- Understand the concept of self-development

Self-leadership gained importance in the context of current organizational changes and newly developed agile leadership approaches (Bracht, Junker, & van Dick, 2018). Until now, the concept of self-leadership has focused on individual-level or team-level goal achievement and is thereby not fully applicable to the broader socio-organizational context (Bracht, Junker, & van Dick, 2018). Self-leading individuals will demonstrate a higher commitment to their tasks, goals, teams, or organizations than individuals who do not engage in self-leadership (Jooste & Frantz, 2017). To understand self-leadership, one needs to have insight into how a leader classifies higher education, whether the role is formal or informal, whether the leader exerts an intentional influence or is determined by context, and how leadership embodies in individuals (Jooste & Frantz, 2017).

Self-leadership in academics fundamentally refers to driven motivation and self-influence to direct oneself towards achieving optimum performance in a situation (Jooste & Frantz, 2017). Self-leadership can be a human resource development-driven. Self-influence can influence self-esteem and life satisfaction (Jooste & Frantz, 2017). In self-leadership, individuals use a series of cognitive, behavioral, and emotional strategies to control their behaviors (Jooste & Frantz, 2017). Studies have demonstrated that self-leadership strategies positively affect individuals' lives (Uzman & Maya, 2019). Self-leadership strategies contribute to participants' effectiveness in problem-solving (Uzman & Maya, 2019).

Self-leadership shows a full mediating effect on the relationships between participating in knowledge-sharing activities and opportunity exploration and idea championing, respectively (Asurakkody & Kim, 2020). To improve innovative work behavior, programs should integrate self-leadership development courses and provide exciting opportunities to gain and share knowledge. This research's results will help organize an integrated program for enhancing self-leadership skills and increasing innovative capabilities (Asurakkody & Kim, 2020). Self-leadership refers to an idea and action strategy that employees use to influence themselves (Kim & Kim, 2019). Self-leadership supports job embeddedness, which is the degree to which a member seeks to remain employed in an organization (Kim & Kim, 2019). Self-leadership positively affects individual and team performance through self-efficacy and job satisfaction (Kim & Kim, 2019).

Self-leadership and human resource factors guide efficient management efficiency (Kim & Kim, 2019). An embodied systems approach to well-being provides further motivation against the fixed mind's notion, pushing self-leadership as perpetual lifespan growth across all sides (Efthimiou, 2017). The study suggests that some leaders maintain healthy working conditions and encourage self-care for themselves and their followers (Klug, Felfe, & Krick, 2019). Health-oriented leadership distinguishes between leaders' and followers' respective concerns for their health regarding self-leadership and leaders' situation for their followers' staff care (Klug, Felfe, & Krick, 2019). A leader's self-care is a favorable precondition for engaging in employee care, because leaders who have strategies to care may transfer them more quickly to their followers (Klug, Felfe, & Krick, 2019).

Self-Assessment

One of the primary elements of self-leadership is self-assessment, meaning to enhance oneself and empower people to embrace their individualism (Ukessays, 2018). Many studies on self-assessment focus on the role of self-assessment in self-leadership and how the concept can improve the organization's performance and the leaders (Ukessays, 2018). According to Van Hala, Cochella, Jaggi, Frost, Kiraly, Pohl, and Gren (2018), individuals need validated instruments to measure progress and target educational interventions to cultivate leadership skills. This idea means that a benchmark must be set to ascertain the credibility and validity of the program. Van Hala et al. (2018) maintain that the leadership self-assessment process can provide content validity for the items presented in the initial tool, using the leaders' collective expertise and feedback from the intended users. Hunt, Heilman, Shutran, and Wu (2017) posit that self-assessment and the awareness of personality traits, behavioral tendencies, and challenges appear to be critical knowledge for those seeking to acquire or improve leadership skills. Incorporating self-assessment into leadership development programs has always proved successful (Hunt et al., 2017).

To improve and increase innovative work behavior, organizations can integrate self-leadership development courses in their training curriculum to provide exciting opportunities for gaining and sharing knowledge.

Self-assessment helps individuals understand themselves better and highlight their personality, behavior, skills, talents, strengths, and weaknesses, among other attributes that effectively help individuals carry out the self-leadership role (Ukessays, 2018). Self-assessment involves self-study by identifying an individual's capabilities and other preferences. Using self-assessment strategically in self-leadership can increase the leader's motivation and engagement and help pinpoint the areas the individual needs to develop and improve themselves (Ukessays, 2018). The design of leadership learning programs enhances the effort to establish what individuals know and do not yet know about their leadership competencies (Lovett & Robertson, 2017). For instance, participants receive personalized feedback reports on their current competencies involving individualized coaching, supports ongoing reflection, and skill development for those learning to lead (Lovett & Robertson, 2017). This claim means that self-assessment interview data from leaders and their experienced leaders can establish the extent to which this self-assessment is a valuable component of leadership learning programs

Self-discovery. There is an emphasis on the need for continuing the journey of self-discovery and self-development (Heizmann & Liu, 2018). Self-discovery depicts a reflective process (Heizmann & Liu, 2018). An essential aspect of sustainability leadership's discursive construction is the unique vision and set of strengths and abilities individuals bring to their future endeavors (Heizmann & Liu, 2018). A leader's self-discovery might inspire others to reflect on their cultural strengths and rise to power positions (Roysircar, Thompson, & Boudreau, 2017). Self-discovery and leadership are bound to a collective self-concept by which leadership can take place both individually and collectively (Roysircar, Thompson, & Boudreau, 2017). Self-identification leads to self-discovery and leadership directions (Roysircar, Thompson, & Boudreau, 2017). Self-discovery leads to the emergence of a conceptual framework, building quality teaching and learning (Gasston-Holmes, 2019).

Self-discovery is a leader of learning, which led to the emergence of a conceptual framework, building capacity for quality teaching, and leading for learning (Gasston-Holmes, 2019). Principals should view middle leaders as agents for change and learning leaders to build a quality teaching and learning framework (Gasston-Holmes, 2019). Self-discovery leads to self-reflection, self-awareness, understanding of the critical role leaders play in collaboration, and building authenticity and trust within any learning environment and organization (Gasston-Holmes, 2019). In the context of self-discovery, leadership goes beyond coaching or mentoring; leadership becomes about developing a professional, trusted relationship that enables a leader to discover themselves, how the leader learns, and how the leader grows professionally, by challenging the predispositions, assumptions, and beliefs (Gasston-Holmes, 2019).

Self-acceptance. Self-acceptance involves the absolute belief in the power of knowledge and self-reflection (Hasberry, 2019). Individuals with high self-acceptance are more confident in accomplishing their goals (Hasberry, 2019). Self-acceptance has a direct, positive influence on negative emotions, availability, social, physical, and positive self-efficacy (Hasberry, 2019). According to Hasberry (2019), a significant relationship exists between self-acceptance and self-esteem (Hasberry, 2019). Self-acceptance has a direct, positive influence on attitudes (Arli & Sutanto, 2018). Self-acceptance is the extent to which self-concept is congruent with an individual's interpretation of the ideal self and the willingness to confront ego-alien and ego-syntonic aspects of the self and accept rather than deny their existence (Arli & Sutanto, 2018). A study suggests that people can take active ownership of their careers as part of a self-acceptance process (Athanasopoulou, Moss-Cowan, Smets, & Morris, 2018).

For an individual to reach a level of self-acceptance in which they see such trade-offs as positive requires work (Athanasopoulou et al., 2018). A leader must take primary responsibility for raising families by taking time off full-time work (Athanasopoulou et al., 2018). For instance, self-acceptance emerges when an individual has to overcome the confidence barriers to develop as a leader (Athanasopoulou et al., 2018). Self-acceptance was a necessary first step on their leadership path, but self-development and self-management were iterative and ongoing (Athanasopoulou et al., 2018). A study suggests that self-acceptance excludes a global human value assessment while maintaining a critical attitude (Popov, 2019). Self-acceptance is a continuum or an intellectual and emotional habit that expresses a greater or lesser level in different individuals (Popov, 2019). Self-acceptance represents an absence of the leader's tendency to globally evaluate their self-worth or ability to accept oneself fully (Popov, 2019).

Self-management. Very little research has directly examined the effectiveness of self-management in comparison to hierarchical leadership in teams. Team characteristics play a different role in the effectiveness of self-managing versus hierarchical leadership structures (Nederveen Pieterse, Hollenbeck, van Knippenberg, Spitzmüller,

Dimotakis, Karam, & Sleesman, 2019). The lack of comparison to high authority differentiation teams presents difficulties in concluding the conditions under which self-management is effective (Nederveen Pieterse et al., 2019). Self-management is vital and requires lifestyle changes, and lifestyle modification self-management programs are more effective; self-efficacy is necessary for optimal self-management (Palacios, Lee, Duaso, Clifton, Norman, Richards, & Barley, 2017). Self-management can positively affect an increased sense of ownership (Palacios et al., 2017).

Depending on the extent to which team members align their efforts, teamwork strategies may serve as a substitute for leadership (Nederveen Pieterse et al., 2019). On the other hand, Smith (2018) provided a better understanding of how leaders should coach in unsupportive environments and offered some fascinating insight into the impact of a hostile environment on managerial coaching. Sawin, Weiss, Johnson, Gralton, Malin, Klingbeil, and Schiffman (2017) view self-management as the ability to resolve competing goals, develop confidence, and manage the external condition. Sawin et al. (2017) emphasized that self-regulation is an iterative problem-solving process, including skills and abilities such as goal setting, self-monitoring, decision-making, planning, and self-evaluation. All individuals involved in developing skills also deal with the evolving issues in the organization.

Self-development. Self-development is also known as personal development, with the manager taking primary responsibility for their learning (Shirbagi, 2018). Self-development is an approach that emphasizes the importance of lifelong learning (Shirbagi, 2018). Self-development recognizes that we all have great potential for learning and changing what we do, and self-development has become the core of successful professional development (Shirbagi, 2018). Self-development is self-motivated and future-oriented. Self-development captures behaviors such as utilizing feedback and setting long-term developmental goals (Zhou, Mao, & Tang, 2020). Leaders must develop benevolent leadership skills to strengthen the relationship between learning from failures and self-development (Zhou, Mao & Tang, 2020). When leaders show benevolent behaviors, employees are inclined to build trust and harmonious interpersonal relationships with their leaders (Zhou, Mao, & Tang, 2020).

The purpose of self-development is for career development and advancement, to improve performance in the current job, to develop specific qualities or skills, and achieve total potential-self-actualization (Shirbagi, 2018). Self-development indicates an employee's self-motivated tendency to achieve progress. As stated earlier, supporting employee development is fundamental in today's dynamic business environment, and employees must adopt the habit of engaging in self-development which is self-motivated and future-oriented. Self-development captures behaviors such as utilizing feedback and setting long-term developmental goals (Zhou, Mao, & Tang, 2020). Benevolent leaders understand how to deal with failure through lessons learned in the process of self-development (Zhou, Mao, & Tang, 2020). Leaders must show benevolent behaviors to inspire employees to build trust and harmonious interpersonal relationships required for team building (Zhou, Mao, & Tang, 2020).

The development process is for preparation for the leadership role and as leaders grow into the role (Athanasopoulou, Moss-Cowan, Smets, & Morris, 2018). For instance, some leaders deliberate on developing big-picture capabilities associated with the strategic skills needed to perform the leadership job (Athanasopoulou et al., 2018). Leaders can create networks to build knowledge and human capital rather than political capital (Athanasopoulou et al., 2018). Extract from Thomas Jefferson to Maria Cosway, on October 12, 1786, "For assuredly nobody will care for him who cares for nobody. But friendship is precious not only in the shade but in the sunshine of life: and thanks to a benevolent arrangement of things, the greater part of life is sunshine." According to Lao Tzu, "When virtue is lost, benevolence appears; when benevolence is lost, right conduct appears; when right conduct is lost, expedience appears. Expediency is the mere shadow of right and truth."

Benevolence (slightly narrower term)
- Action intended to benefit another, but **not to gain external reward**)

CHAPTER 7

SELF-LEADERSHIP ANALYSIS

Learning Objectives:

- Understand self-leader perceptions

- Identify the barriers to self-leadership

- Understand how self-leadership supports team-building

- The benefit of self-leadership training

The TEAM LEAD model enhances the body of knowledge related to self-leadership and team building. Also, it addresses the influence of self-leadership in team building among leaders and the discussion of leaders' experiences and the perception of self-leadership. Interviews were conducted to better understand the participant's perceptions of self-leadership using the Interview Guide designed to establish the research's parameters and scope.

All leaders invited to participate in the research study were carefully chosen from convenience sampling. The participants were current or former supervisors and employees leading a team or program. These participants have also taken part in a government-sponsored leadership development program (LDP) in the last five years. Participants in the research could either be currently enrolled in an LDP or training. The leaders who participated in a Leadership Development Program are either leading a program or a team. The participants answered seventeen questions regarding self-leadership and team-building experiences.

During the interviews, participants also addressed the benefit of having a leadership development program in an organization. Also, participants discussed the benefit of having self-leadership training and the influence of self-leadership on team building. Participants answered questions on their leadership style and their supervisors' current and former influence on their professional growth. The leaders who participated in a government-sponsored Leadership Development Program or training believe that the training helped in their self-leadership skills. These participants agreed that self-leadership training influenced their team-building abilities as leaders. Also, follow-up questions were asked to obtain additional information from the participants when applicable.

The data collection commenced by conducting structured interviews with team leads and program leads. These interviews consisted of Part A (Research Question 1) and Part B (Research Question 2). After analyzing the data collected during the interview process, multiple themes were identified, contributing to the body of knowledge in self-leadership. Additionally, multiple themes were identified to support the research questions highlighted in Section 1. The themes identified during the data collection and analysis include the following:

- Leadership competence: The ability to be a better supervisor and have improved leadership ability for effective decision-making.
- Human skill: The ability to understand people; this type of leadership skill will help the leader to better understand the people.
- Self-leadership: Self-leadership training keeps leaders conscious of applying what they learn by implementing leadership skills—self-leadership training helps them learn and reinforce gratefulness values.
- Professional skill: Leadership training can help leaders in making the right decision in the work environment. Having professional skills gives leaders access to effective decision-making.
- Self-development: Training obtained from adapting to various leadership styles makes it possible to successfully

overcome negativity when you develop yourself as a leader, focusing on positivity.
- Team orientation: This means being able to navigate daily crises as a team. Self-leadership puts one in charge of their progress and allows them to keep a record of where they lack. The second initial code for this theme is conflict management. This activity gives a leader access to constructive feedback.

One additional theme that emerged from the study but that was not specified in alignment with Research Question 1 in Part A included:
- Learning and growth: This means that having a self-leadership program will enable a leader's personal and professional development. This concept should be the foundation for organizational strategy and focus on the employees and emerging leaders to develop leadership capacity.

Self-leadership Perceptions

The themes anticipated from this research study include developing empathy as a self-leadership trait, building social skills, and self-regulation. The ability to influence team members and be accountable to the team, having the team-building ability, self-leadership training, management skills, and individual understanding barriers and organizational barriers prevents a leader from building a cohesive team. Continuous learning and self-development supported by the organization, having improved people skills, team efficacy, enhanced knowledge and skills, enhanced leadership propensity to lead self, and perceived value of self-leadership training as the core ability for organizational success. Leaders must first lead themselves before leading others.

An additional theme to discuss is the proposal to make self-leadership training a mandatory requirement for leaders. The perception is that to be considered for any leadership position in the organization, the person must acquire self-leadership training. Those individuals must have participated in a government-sponsored leadership development training where self-leadership is part of the leadership course curriculum.

Making self-leadership training mandatory is designed to reduce failure and ensure that every leader complies with the policy and guidance.

Evaluation of the Findings

Interviews were conducted with 20 study participants using the Interview Guide found in Appendix A. Some of the study participants were current or former employees of the federal government. All the participants were leading a program or leading a team of people. Three of the 20 participants were in the GG-15 pay grade; nine were in the GG-14 pay grade; seven were in the GG-13 pay grade; one was in the GG-12 pay grade. The race of all participants was not relevant for this research and was not considered.

Table 2 - Participants rank representation

Description of Participants	Number	Percentage
Rank of GG-15	3	15
Rank of GG-14	9	45
Rank of GG-13	7	35
Rank of GG-12	1	5

Each participant had undergone government-sponsored leadership development training within the last five years of their career in the federal government. This analysis was divided into part a, the RQ1, and part b, the RQ2.

RQ 1: Part A – Question on how self-leadership supports team building. Out of 20, eighteen people participated in the government-sponsored leadership Development Program (LDP) in the last five years. In contrast, two respondents did not participate in the LDP training but took part in other government training.

Table 3 - Participants in a Govt-Sponsored LDP

Description of Participants	Number	Percentage
Govt-Sponsored LDP	18	90
Other Leadership Training	2	10
Non-Govt. LDP	0	0

One respondent said that LDP training had helped their promotion in the last five years by enhancing their leadership skills; twelve participants said the training program did not help them get promoted. Five respondents stated that they were offered new positions after the completion of LDP. One respondent noted that it helped them reinforce concepts. Another respondent mentioned that the LDP training program helped them understand leadership's importance.

Table 4 - Participants that benefited from LDP training

Description of Participants	Number	Percentage
Benefits from the LDP	1	5
Benefits from other training	7	35
No Benefit from LDP	12	60

Eleven respondents stated that LDP training was an option, whereas nine respondents thought it was a requirement. Nine respondents mentioned that LDP training was conducted online and in-class; seven respondents said it was conducted online. In contrast, four respondents noted that the training was conducted in class. Three respondents responded no to self-leadership as part of the LDP curriculum, whereas seventeen responded yes.

Table 5 - The participant with an option for LDP training

Description of Participants	Number	Percentage
LDP as an option	11	5
LDP as requirement	9	35
LDP conducted in class	0	0

Table 6 - Participant on how the LDP was conducted

Description of Participants	Number	Percentage
LDP conducted on both	9	45
LDP conducted online	7	35
LDP conducted in class	4	20

Table 7 - Participant in self-leadership in the curriculum

Description of Participants	Number	Percentage
No response	0	0
Not in the curriculum	3	35
Self-leadership curriculum	17	20

Thirteen of the respondents said their current supervisors did not go through the LDP training before their promotion to their current role; four respondents said their current supervisors went through the LDP training, while three did not know about this. The data analysis shows that the respondents' opinions about the benefits of having a leader who has undergone the LDP training are divided into four themes: a - Leadership Competency, b- Human Skills, c-Self-leadership, and d - Professional Skills.

The first theme, Leadership Competency, further discusses three initial codes. The first initial code for this theme is how to be a better supervisor. Participant_1 stated that one of the benefits of the LDP training program is that it teaches the supervisor how to improve their leadership skills. The second initial code for this theme is improved leadership ability. Participant_2 shares that the LDP training can improve leadership ability by making them more productive. In Participant_2's words, "If they were to utilize the training received in LDP and apply it to the real-time scenario, I would wonder if their leadership abilities would have been different and more productive."

The third initial code for this theme is situational oversight. The leadership competency is increased as the training aid in the handling of decision-making and situational oversight; as Participant_3 mentioned, "I was able to see the differences these things made in my leadership in both how they handled decision-making, situational oversight, and personnel situations." The second theme is Human Skills. The first initial code for this theme is understanding people; Participant_4 stated that leadership training can help leaders better understand the people.

The second initial code for this theme is caring for others. Participant_5 mentioned that this training program could effectively help the leaders in caring for themselves and others. The third initial code for this theme is collaborations. Participant_6 commented that leadership training could help the leader expand their network for possible future collaborations. The fourth initial code for this theme is the ability to manage people. Participant_7 responded that the training program is effective for new leaders, "for a new leader, the program is beneficial because it teaches the individual how to lead and manage people to maximize their potential." The third theme is self-leadership; the first initial code for this theme is identifying strengths and weaknesses. Participant_8 stated that the training program could help self-leadership by allowing people to identify their strengths and shortfalls.

The second initial code for this theme is a sense of responsibility. This training program can induce a sense of responsibility among the new leaders. Participant_9 mentioned that "leaders must have a sense of responsibility to be effective as leaders." The third initial code for this theme is shared understanding. Participant_10 shared that the leadership program can help new leaders understand what it means to be a leader. The fourth theme is professional skills. The first initial code for this theme is effective decision-making. Participant_11 shared that leadership training can help the leaders make the right decision in the work environment.

> *One of the benefits of the LDP training program is that it teaches the supervisor how to improve their leadership skills. Training programs could help self-leadership by allowing people to identify their strengths and shortfalls.*

The second initial code for this theme is gaining knowledge. One of the respondents stated that formal training and gaining experience is essential for a leader to work skillfully in a professional environment. The third initial code for this theme is improved communication. Participant_11 stated that leaders must learn effective communication through the training program to make their leadership effective. Participant_11 agrees with the literature review notion by Kharouf et al. (2019) that effective communication plays a vital role in building and maintaining long-term relationships. The fourth initial code for this theme is professionalism. Participant_12 shared that the training program can lead to professionalism and fairness.

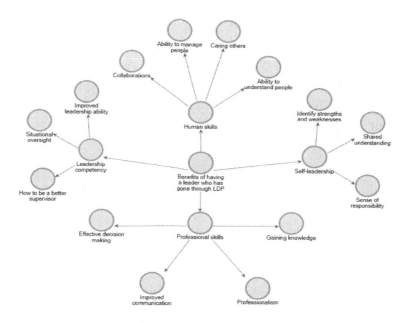

Figure 4. Benefits of having a leader with LDP training.

The data shows that the respondents' opinions about the benefits of having self-leadership training can be divided into three themes: a - Self-development, b- Team orientation, and c - Learning and growth.

The First theme, self-development, is further divided into seven initial codes; the first initial code for this theme is the ability to self-lead. Participant_13 mentioned that self-leadership training is essential for self-development, as it is beneficial in situations where the leader cannot perform their duty successfully. The second initial code for this theme is applying what is learned. A respondent mentioned that self-leadership training keeps one conscious of using what they learn and self-implementing the training. The third initial code for this theme is to learn and reinforce value.

Participant_14 responded that "self-leadership training helps to learn and reinforce gratefulness and thankfulness values." The fourth initial code for this theme is learning self-accountability. Participant_15 mentioned that "self-leadership training help in taking accountability for one's actions." The fifth initial code for this theme is self-Improvement. A respondent shared that this training program can help in self-reflection and self-improvement. The sixth initial code for this theme is self-motivation. In the words of Participant_16, this training program "provides self-motivation for your career and work products." The seventh initial code for this theme is understanding personal strengths and weaknesses.

The self-leadership program helps a person understand their strengths and weaknesses. The second theme is team orientation. The first initial code for this theme is to develop leadership skills. In the words of Participant_17, "self-leadership training allows leaders to learn about their skillset and develop the mindset they need to lead subordinates." The second initial code for this theme is seeking constructive feedback. Participant_18 mentioned that a self-leadership program develops team orientation and gives a person access to constructive feedback. The third initial code for this theme is team building. Participant_19 noted that a self-leadership program could induce a team-building spirit.

The third theme is learning and growth. The first initial code for this theme is to enhance knowledge. Participant_20 responded that a self-leadership program enhances one's knowledge and, more importantly, gives space for applying what one has learned. Participant_20's answer supports the assertion in the literature review by Bendell, Sullivan, and Marvel (2019), suggesting that some self-leadership strategies are helpful when applied to high-growth entrepreneurship. The second initial code for this theme is personal and professional growth. This self-leadership program aids in personal and professional development. The third initial code for this theme is perspective on leadership styles. In the words of a respondent, "Well, I think it gives you a greater perspective on different leadership styles and techniques."

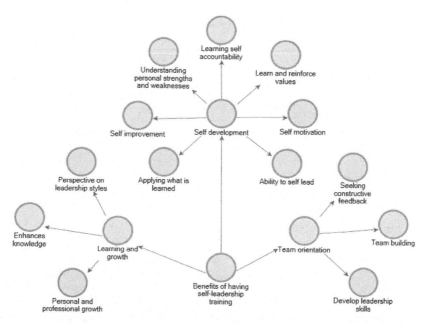

Figure 5. Benefits of having Self-leadership training for leaders.

Seventeen respondents say their organization does not mandate self-leadership training for supervisors, whereas only three said their organization does. Participant_17 mentioned that self-leadership helps the teams in resolving issues. Participant_18 noted that self-leadership improves the ability to make use of self-strength. Participant_19 indicated that self-leadership helps in improving communication. Three respondents said that self-leadership should not be a requirement in their organization. In contrast, eleven respondents said it should be. One respondent mentioned that they have an authoritarian leadership style. Three respondents said they have a democratic leadership style. One other respondent mentioned they have a Laissez-Faire leadership style. Six respondents have a servant leadership style, two have a situational leadership style, and four said they have a transformational leadership style.

Table 8 - Leadership styles

Leadership Style	Frequency
Authoritarian leadership style	1
Democratic leadership style	3
Laissez-Faire style	1
Servant leader	6
Situational leadership	2
Transformational leader	4

Five out of 20 participants said no, they do not identify any leader as a positive role model, while fifteen said yes. Nine out of 20 respondents said no, they do not have a mentor, while eleven participants said yes, they did. Three respondents said no, their mentors did not create goals, whereas eight participants said yes. Two people said their mentors did not guide them in reaching their goals; ten respondents said they did. Participant_19 said that their mentor influences or inspires them to achieve their goals through constant communication. Participant_20 said they did it through encouragement. One respondent said their mentor influenced or inspired them through motivation. Two of the respondents mentioned that their mentors did not inspire or influence them at all. Eight of the participants responded yes. Three of the respondents said no, their mentors did not intellectually challenge them with new perspectives and ideas; nine of the participants responded yes. The data analysis shows that respondents' perceptions and views on how self-leadership influenced their team building can be divided into five themes: a- Empathy, b- Social skills, c- Self-regulation, d- Influence on team members, e- Team orientation.

The first initial code for the first theme is being mindful of others. Self-leadership teaches one to listen more and speak less, which leads to being more mindful of others. The second initial code for this theme is building trust and respecting others. Participant_15 mentioned that self-leadership has helped build trust and respect faster, which is pivotal to success. The third initial code for this theme is the realization that everyone can be a leader. Self-leadership teaches that everyone can become a leader, regardless of their duty title or grade. The second theme is social skills; the first initial code for this theme is appreciating. Self-leadership allows an individual to appreciate diversity which leads to the building of a high-performance team.

The second initial code for this theme is relationship building. Self-leadership teaches relationship building which is vital in team dynamics. The third theme is self-regulation; the first initial code is leading a team by example. Self-leadership enables the leader to lead by example rather than dictating. The second initial code for this theme is looking for positive ways. Participant_16 mentioned that "my self-leadership consisted of looking for positive ways to make or perform something better." The next theme is influence on team members; the first initial code addresses preconceptions and biases. Self-leadership allows leaders to influence their team members positively. The second initial code for this theme is to build credibility. Self-leadership gives credibility to leaders when their followers observe their capability.

The third initial code for this theme is to influence the team members. Participant_16 stated that "when I was in the team lead role, my self-leadership gave me strength and know-how to influence my team to give their all, and with that my team completed assignments on time." The next theme is team orientation; the first initial code is to navigate daily crises as a team. Self-leadership puts one in charge of their progress and allows them to keep a record of where they lack. The second initial code for this theme is conflict management. Self-leaderships enable a leader to understand the situation better and enhance their management skills.

The third initial code for this theme is meeting team goals. It helps the leaders to be more successful in meeting their goals. The fourth initial code for this theme is motivating team members. Participant_17 mentioned, "actively paying attention to what motivates them and providing them the support they need to be successful in moving the mission forward." The fifth initial code for this theme is understanding strengths and weaknesses. For instance, Participant_18 agrees with Zaech and Baldegger (2017) that leaders appeal to their followers' self-interest to motivate them to achieve specific tasks. A respondent stated that "self-leadership has allowed me to understand my strengths and where I need improvement."

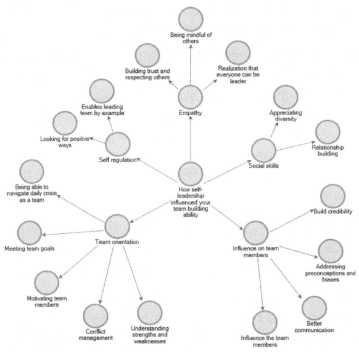

Figure 6. How self-leadership influences team building.

The data analysis shows respondents' perceptions and views on how their self-leadership enhanced their organization's growth and overall business success; this is divided into three themes: a- Self-regulation and accountability, b- Team building, and c - Management skills.

The first initial code for self-regulation is enhancing mission accomplishment. Participant_17 stated that "what things I can thrive in and help the organization as a whole achieve its goals and mission." The second initial code for this theme is a sense of accountability.

Accountability to one's word and the teammates enhances the overall growth of the organization. The second theme is team building. The first initial code for this theme is building respect and trust. Self-leadership training enables an individual to build trust in the process and establish a relationship with their co-workers.

The second initial code for this theme is building trust with team members. Participant_18 stated that "being honest with your word allows a trust component to be built and can bring the team to recognize you not only care about the mission but the team's success as a whole." The third initial code for this theme is the empowerment of the team. Self-leadership prepares an individual to remove roadblocks and support the team, empowering them to perform better. The fourth initial code for this theme is team orientation.

One of the respondents mentioned that "I believe this approach has been successful in building teams within my business units and has contributed to my success in business management." The third theme is management skills; the first initial code for this theme is enhancing communication. Self-leadership increases the communication competency of an individual. The second initial code for this theme is problem-solving. Participant_19 mentioned that "problem-solving at the leading self-level directly correlates to strategic thinking at the leading the institution level." Participant_19 agrees with Uzman and Maya (2019) in the literature review that self-leadership strategies contribute to participants' effectiveness in problem-solving.

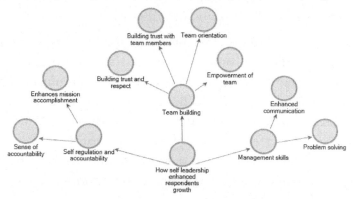

Figure 7. It shows how self-leadership enhances organizational growth.

None of the respondents said that they would not recommend adopting the concept of self-leadership to emerging leaders in their current organization; all twenty of them said yes. Participant_20 said they do not consider themself as a leader; one of them said 'somewhat;' eighteen of the respondents said they think of themselves as leaders.

RQ 2/Part B - Discusses barriers to self-leadership in team building. Participant_1 characterized the concept of self-leadership in their organization to apply leadership concepts in practice; seven respondents were not sure; one responded with "seeking opportunities;" and another said that self-leadership is individual responsibility. The barriers to the self-leadership attributes in an organization are divided into two themes: a - Individual barriers, and b - Organizational barriers.

The first initial code for the first theme is the self-imposed barriers. Some barriers that come in the way of self-leadership can be self-imposed that halt growth and development. The second initial code for this theme is lack of communication. Participant_2 responded that lack of communication is the barrier to self-leadership attributes in their organization. The third initial code for this theme is the lack of implementation of learning. Participant_3 stated that,

> "My organization has not implemented a method for ensuring training offered or acquired is utilized to its max, where the right people get the training because no time is set aside to attend the training (usually online), as it is left up to individuals to work it into their regular work hours if they can."

The fourth initial code for this theme is a leader who is not open to new ideas. Another barrier to self-leadership attributes is a leader that does not invite new ideas into the work environment. The fifth initial code for this theme is a leader who does not have the employee's best interest. Leaders who do not look after their employees and do not consider their feedback is another kind of barrier. The sixth initial code for this theme is micro-management. Another barrier is micro-management, which keeps the teams from performing their jobs and learning from their mistakes.

The seventh initial code for this theme is not applying emotional intelligence to problem-solving. Participant_4 stated that "some barriers I have experienced are not asking the right questions and not applying emotional intelligence to the problem at hand." The eighth initial code for this theme is outdated leadership traits. Outdated leadership traits also hinder self-leadership by keeping the organizational culture from adapting to modernity. The second theme is organizational barriers. The first initial code for this theme is a lack of funding for initiatives. Lack of monetary support can come off as a barrier in the way of self-leadership.

The second initial code for this theme is a limited opportunity. Limited or lack of opportunity to exercise the learned skill is another barrier in the process. The third initial code for this theme is nationality. Participant_5 responded that "the biggest barrier of self-leadership in my organization is nationality; our none diversified leadership reflects that fact." The fourth initial code for this theme is no leadership encouragement. Another barrier is a lack of encouragement from the organization.

The fifth initial code for this theme is organizational culture. Outdated leadership traits at a senior level come off as another barrier in the process. The sixth initial code for this theme is work-life balance. Lack of work-life balance can also halt self-leadership; Participant_6 stated that "I think an important part of self-leadership is directly tied to a good work-life balance, and I think that in itself could be a barrier within my organization."

Image adapted from Human Resources online

The Team Lead Model of Self-Leadership

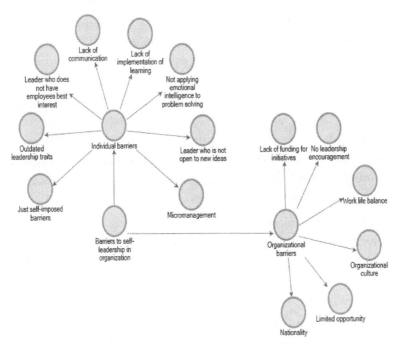

Figure 8. *Barriers to Self-leadership attributes.*

The respondents' responses to how they overcome any self-leadership barrier in their organization can be divided into three themes: a - Learning and self-development, b- Improved people skills, and c - Self-regulation.

The first initial code for the theme of learning and self-development is adapting different leadership styles. Adapting a variety of different leadership styles makes it possible to overcome negativity. The second initial code for this theme is the focus on positivity. Participant_7 shared that they focus on the positive outcomes instead of the negative outcomes. I realize that I can't change everything, so I have learned to focus on things within my sphere of influence and accept what I cannot change."

The third initial code for this theme is self-reflection. Taking the time to do self-reflection overcomes self-leadership barriers. The fourth initial code for this theme is training and education. Leaders can overcome these barriers by training in educating those who work for them. The second theme is improved people skills. The first initial code for this theme is trusting people. Trust building is essential to overcome the self-leadership barriers; the staff must come to the leader and discuss their concerns.

The second initial code for this theme is understanding that people are different. Understanding that not everyone has the same work ethic is another way to improve people skills and overcome self-leadership barriers. The third theme is self-regulation; the first initial code for this theme is a sense of accountability. Recognition of what one is accountable for can help in overcoming the barrier. The second initial code for this theme is striving for goals. Continuing striving for goals and hoping for things to fall into their place eventually is a way of self-regulation that can help overcome self-leadership barriers.

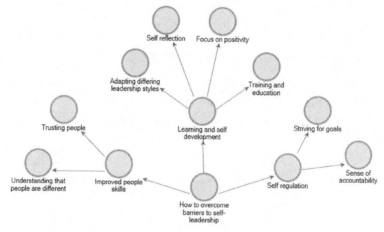

Figure 9. Shows how to overcome self-leadership barriers.

Table 9 – Responses on how to overcome self-leadership barriers

Representative Statements from Interviews	Initial Codes	Themes
By adopting different leadership styles and focusing on constantly varying self-leadership attributes, it is sometimes possible to overcome negativity more successfully.	Adapting differing leadership styles	
I focus on the positives. I realize that I can't change everything, so I have learned to focus on things within my sphere of influence and accept what I cannot change.	Focus on positivity	Learning and self-development
Taking the time to do self-reflection	Self-reflection	
Leaders are willing to let you get training and education.	Training and Education	
You have to trust your staff to be willing to come to you when they see something. Ultimately, you need trust.	Trusting people	Improved people skills
You have to understand that not everyone has the same work ethic to their work productively.	Understanding that people are different	
Recognize that I can only be accountable for what I can control	Sense of accountability	Self-regulation
Continue striving for my goals and hope that things will fall in place eventually.	Striving for goals	

In describing the prevalence of self-leadership in their organization, Participant_8 mentioned that there are "self-leaders at different organizational levels." Six respondents stated that self-leadership is not focused in their organization. Fifteen respondents had the opportunity to participate in leadership development programs before their promotion to a leadership position; three did not. Eight respondents did not consider seeking self-leadership training in their new leadership role; nine stated they did. The analysis of the highlighted benefits of having self-leadership training for the team members is further divided into three themes: a - Team efficacy, b- Enhanced knowledge and skills, and c - Enhanced leadership propensity.

In the first theme, team efficacy, the first initial code is improved work environment. A self-leadership training program helps in achieving a more productive and friendly work environment. The second initial code for this theme is increased effectiveness. This training program allows all team members to have a common starting point, which increases teamwork effectiveness. The third initial code for this theme is a sense of working in a team. It teaches the individuals the right way to work in a team. The fourth initial code is to have enhanced knowledge by speaking a common language. Through the same training, the team members speak the same language and better understand each other. The fifth initial code for this theme is to understand the importance of self in the team. Participant_11 shared, "It would allow them to understand the importance of self and how the word "self" is the missing piece of a successful team."

The sixth initial code for this theme is understanding strengths and weaknesses. The self-leadership training programs allow one to understand their strengths and weakness. The next theme is enhanced knowledge and skills; the first initial code is decision-making skills. Participant_12 stated that one of the best outcomes of this training program is improved decision-making skills. The second initial code for this theme is self-awareness. Self-awareness is a crucial element of team building. The third initial code for this theme is self-improvement.

Participant_13 mentioned that "we are working together to improve ourselves, so it is a team effort. It benefits not only the organization but also their family and is useful for the rest of their life." Participant_13 highlights the significance of team building, as emphasized by Ireland et al. (2017) that team-building activities provide employees the feeling that belonging to their workgroup is vital. The fourth initial code for this theme is understanding perspectives. These training programs allow the team members to address their shortcomings and understand the views of other team members. The fifth initial code for this theme is understanding the role of personality in decision-making. Participant_14 mentioned that "the first thing is, the training will teach you about who you are and how your personality can drive decisions you make as a leader."

For the third theme, enhancing leadership propensity, the first initial code is confidence to lead the team. Through this training program, every team member acquires the trust of leading their team at any given time. The second initial code for this theme is developing people to become leaders. This training also developed the people in the right direction and set them off to become leaders themselves. The third initial code for this theme is the foundation of leadership training. Participant_15 responded that "it should be the foundation for any other leadership training and for being an effective leader."

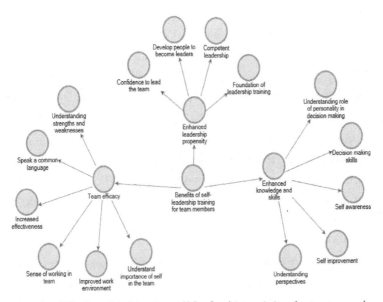

Figure 10. The benefit of having self-leadership training for team members.

The analysis of the respondents' perceptions and views on establishing self-leadership training is further divided into three themes: a- Perceived value, b- Proposed design, and c - Views to make it a mandatory requirement.

The first initial code for the theme of perceived value is considering it a priority. The importance of this training program must be established as a priority. The second initial code for this theme is what is good for employees. This training program has a lot of benefits for the participants. The third initial code for this theme is necessary for talent development. Self-leadership programs are a necessity for the development of talent building. The fourth initial code for this theme is paramount to the organization. Participant_16 mentioned that "this is paramount for any organization to invest in their employees by providing self-leadership training. It's a good thing even if folks are not seeking leadership roles, we all need to know that first, we are leaders of ourselves."

The fifth initial code for this theme is a positive thing. This training program denotes that the organization cares for and respects the different perspectives of the employees. The sixth initial code for this theme is positive thinking. Participant_17 shared that "It is a positive thing and means that the organization care and you need external training for their employees because they have a different perspective." The seventh initial code for this theme is a valuable tool. Self-leadership training is a helpful tool that allows the participants to add value to the overall organizational structure—the first initial code for the theme proposing the design of an employee development program. The establishment of the self-leadership training program aims at the formation of an employee training program. The second initial code for this theme is a foundational requirement. Participant_19 responded that "it should be a foundational requirement and be provided primarily in a classroom environment with others."

The third initial code for this theme is offering customized training. The self-leadership training provides both organization and individual-specific training. The first initial code for the third theme of view is to make leadership development mandatory, resulting in a mandatory promotion. Some respondents suggested that self-leadership training must be compulsory for everyone who intends to step up the promotion ladder. The second initial code for this theme is non-mandatory. Some other respondents suggested otherwise, e.g., participant_20 stated that "as I previously indicated, my perceptions and views on the establishment of self-leadership training are that it should not be mandatory because not all want to be leaders, not all want the responsibility that comes along with being a leader."

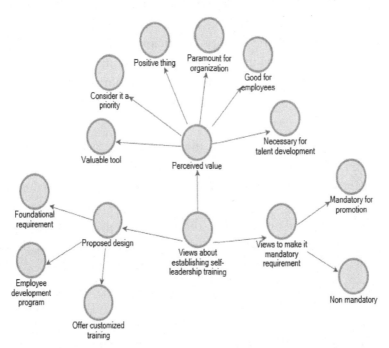

Figure 11. Opinion on establishing self-leadership training.

Data saturation. The data saturation point was within the eighteenth interview. After eighteen interviews, the collected data yielded similar and consistent results. There were no exclusive or distinguishing ideas that occurred after eighteen interviews. Furthermore, no annotations were identified in the last two interviews conducted. Also, no new concepts would be identified in this analysis if the qualitative research interviews were to continue (Gugiu, Randall, Gibbons, Hunter, Naegeli, & Symonds, 2020). The merging of the seven consistent and recurring themes recognized above is an indication of data triangulation. Data triangulation is evidence of optimum authentication of the results of this study. Triangulation comprises various data sources, which can shed light on the same phenomenon (Jentoft & Olsen, 2019). The discussion of the multiple themes supports the research questions posed in Section 1. The seeming themes comprised the following:

Leadership competency. The ability to be a better supervisor and have improved leadership capacity for effective decision-making. The organization performs a needs assessment to collect quantitative and qualitative feedback from participants (Nghe, Hart, Ferry, Hutchins, & Lebet, 2020). Leadership competency provides the structure for developing individuals to move into a higher leadership roles (Nghe et al., 2020). An organization that supports its employees' development gives them access to a broader range of development activities; hence they are more likely to report higher competence levels in qualities and skills (Dawson, Hepworth, Bugaian, & Williams, 2020). Leaders and managers have different leadership competency levels in the skill and quality of service they provide to the organization (Dawson et al., 2020). This notion indicates the importance of having the required self-leadership training or expertise as tools for managing resources and people and the qualities and skills of a leader with leadership competence.

Human skill. The ability to understand people; this type of leadership skill will help the leader better understand the people. It is essential to demonstrate human skills in our engagement with other people to achieve a common goal. Every leader has to improve their soft skills, such as communication, public speaking, and promoting those professional skills by interacting with people (Akverdian, 2019). When discussing professional development, it is critical to developing human skills with tools used for problem-solving. Human talent simply considers the human factor when engaging with others (Evans, Pawlina, & Lachman, 2018). Curricula that once provided students with these basic educational units no longer and should no longer focus solely on knowledge-based competencies but should promote human skills development (Evans, Pawlina, & Lachman, 2018).

Self-leadership training. Self-leadership training keeps leaders conscious of applying what they learn by implementing leadership skills—self-leadership training helps them learn and reinforce gratefulness values. The course of this research establishes that the concept of self-leadership focuses on individual or team-level goal achievement and is thereby not fully applicable to the broader socio-organizational context (Bracht, Junker, & van Dick, 2018). Self-leadership gains importance in the context of current organizational changes, like in newly developed agile methods, where leadership is mainly replaced by self-leadership (Bracht, Junker, & van Dick, 2018). Self-leadership culture positively influences the employee's job satisfaction within a team setting (Bracht, Junker, & van Dick, 2018). Self-leadership plays a crucial role in this context of employees who work periodically in both a traditional office and home office without supervision (Müller & Niessen, 2019). Self-controlling behaviors are crucial in everyday life. For instance, self-control keeps people from over-eating or procrastinating on work tasks; we examined within-person variations in self-leadership (Müller & Niessen, 2019).

Professional skill. Having professional skills gives leaders access to effective decision-making. Leadership training can help the leaders make the right decision in the work environment. Academics' international mobility promotes professional competence and self-awareness (Pylväs & Nokelainen, 2021). This recent study emphasizes the augmentation of creating global networks and enhancing current and future career prospects. (Pylväs & Nokelainen, 2021). The knowledge and skills developed during the academic staff exchange are closely related to generic working life skills (Pylväs & Nokelainen, 2021). Concerning professional development, a recent study highlights the participants' perceived development of generic professional skills, such as self-reflection, problem-solving, and creativity (Pylväs & Nokelainen, 2021). Scholars agree that professional development is crucial for implementing education policies that call for change (Pak, Desimone, & Parsons, 2020). Professional development generally needs to be content-focused, active, collaborative, coherent, and sustained (Pak, Desimone, & Parsons, 2020). Leaders must receive professional development that supports their adaptations to the rigorous teaching and learning expectations embedded in educational standards (Pak, Desimone, & Parsons, 2020).

Self-development. Training obtained from adapting to various leadership styles makes it possible to successfully overcome negativity when leaders develop themselves, focusing on positivity. Leadership educators must strive to develop a training curriculum for future generations of leaders (Armstrong & McCain, 2021). For instance, the classroom must be designed around constructing narratives about oneself, a group, and others to help students develop an authentic leadership voice (Armstrong & McCain, 2021). A leader should not be afraid of failure (Zhou, Mao, & Tang, 2020). Learning from failures is key to effective employee functioning and long-term sustainable development (Zhou, Mao, & Tang, 2020).

Team orientation. Team orientation is the ability to navigate daily crises as a team. Self-leadership puts a person in charge of their progress and allows them to keep a record of where they lack (Müller & Niessen, 2019. This concept gives a leader access to constructive feedback. According to Huang, Jia-Chi, and Chang (2019), teams can be characterized according to all team members' average goal orientation level. A recent study identifies two different goal orientations concerning developing and demonstrating a team's abilities (Huang, Jia-Chi, & Chang, 2019). Team orientation is another communication characteristic that may influence a team (Guznov, Lyons, Pfahler, Heironimus, Woolley, Friedman, & Neimeier, 2020). Team orientation occurs when team members' roles and responsibilities are adjusted based on members' skillsets (Guznov et al., 2020). Communication between team members impacts how roles and responsibilities are allocated (Guznov et al., 2020). Sharing information is critical for team success (Guznov et al., 2020).

Learning and growth. A recent study identifies the importance of learning by targeting the impact of age on growth rates (Arkolakis, Papageorgiou, & Timoshenko, 2018). Learning and growth relate to an organization with a self-leadership program that enables personal and professional development. This idea should be the foundation for organizational strategy and focus on the employees and emerging leaders for developing leadership capacity. According to Arkolakis, Papageorgiou, and Timoshenko (2018), learning affects both the growth and the behavior of an organization. Arkolakis, Papageorgiou, and Timoshenko (2018) developed a framework to evaluate the significance of learning for organizational growth by appropriately adapting a standard learning mechanism. Learning is the critical mechanism that accounts for the professional growth rate. Emde (2020) asserts that high learning rates can have downsides if not aligned with required growth.

Overview of the Findings

This qualitative research case study anticipates answering the research questions posed in Section 1 and contributing to the body of knowledge regarding self-leadership influence in team-building in an organization. This finding was achieved by exploring how self-leadership influences team building. Twenty interviews were conducted using the Interview Guide found in Appendix A. The federal employees who were invited to participate in the study were selected from convenience sampling. There were almost 35 questions that were asked to the respondents, and the respondents answered 25 questions with 'yes' or 'no' to specific questions. The analysis of the questions with yes or no answers was presented in table form with their frequency. Nineteen of the 20 respondents answered the questions in full regarding their self-leadership experiences, team-building ability, leadership styles, barriers encountered during team building, and how to overcome those barriers in the organization.

The participants addressed the influence of self-leadership in team building and how leadership development program influences the growth of individuals, organization, and overall business success. Two respondents were uncertain if self-leadership could influence their team-building ability. The majority of the respondents believed they obtained leadership development training before they moved to their leadership roles. Only three out of the 20 participants were unsure if self-leadership training would have helped them build a cohesive team. Despite the relevance of self-leadership training, six of the 20 respondents believed that self-leadership training is not the focus of their present organization. Recent research shows that self-leadership gains importance in the face of rising complexity and a high speed of development and innovation in today's economy (Bracht, 2019).

In my several professional years of leading people and programs, my view on leadership is that it is a privilege given to a person to serve others with humility and help them achieve a set goal for the betterment of everyone. Leadership is about relationships; that said, a leadership position should not be a platform for people to display their self-importance. Additionally, my interpretation of self-leadership is that it is an opportunity to prove to yourself that you can influence your behavior positively to achieve a personal goal that will benefit both you and the people around you.

Image: Self-Leadership

CHAPTER 8

SELF-LEADERSHIP TRAITS

Learning Objectives:

- Self-leadership traits support leadership competence

- The participants' viewpoint on self-leadership

Self-leadership traits as developed in the TEAM LEAD model identify eight core attributes for effective leadership. The premise is that self-care is a relational leadership trait that people develop due to the desire to achieve personal goals in life conscientiously. A person can predict leadership effectiveness. The findings revealed that openness to experience emerged as the best predictor of leadership effectiveness, followed by conscientiousness (Singh, 2009). The dynamics of a self-pattern are reflected in referencing predictive processing accounts that allow for investigation (Gallagher and Daly, 2018). With the Interview Guide, the questions asked during the research of this book were used to develop the framework for the eight self-leadership behaviors outlined in this TEAM LEAD model that helps a leader become more effective. For instance, participants were asked questions on self-leadership that resulted in listing core self-leadership attributes for leaders in an organization. The initial question was if participants were part of any government-sponsored leadership development program in the last five years. This question helped to ensure that we have the right people participating in this research.

The questions that needed answers. Participants answered the additional question of whether they were in a leadership position. This was the opening question in Part A of the research question, RQ1. The second question was whether the participant's current supervisor went through the LDP training before being promoted to leadership. The third question was whether the participant's organization mandated self-leadership training for supervisors. The fourth question was for participants to describe their leadership style with current team members. The participants identified six leadership styles. Transformational leadership and servant leadership style were the most popular among the participants. According to Curtis (2020), rational thinking and imagination positively correlate with transformational leadership when followers rate leadership and thinking styles rather than self-rated. Harb, Hachem, and Hamdan (2021) emphasized that leadership style is one of the most critical factors in promoting organizational commitment.

The fifth question was for the participants to describe their perceptions and views on how self-leadership influenced team-building ability in their current organizations. Goldsby, Goldsby, Neck, Neck, and Mathews (2021) state that increased self-leadership corresponds with better affective responses and improved team performance. Pillay, Nel, and Harunavamwe (2020) determined that self-leadership strategies (constructive thought patterns, behavioral strategies, and natural rewards) through psychological resources (hope, optimism, and self-efficacy) positively influenced job embeddedness. The sixth question was for the participants to describe their perceptions and views on how individuals' self-leadership enhanced the organization's growth and overall business success.

The seventh question asked if the participants would recommend emerging leaders to adopt the concept of self-leadership in their current organization. According to Wang, Gao, Sun, Liu, and Fan (2021), practicing relative self-leadership strategies may reduce procrastination. Lee, Park, and Choi (2020) suggest that increased self-leadership skills will improve a leader's self-management behavior. Participants' responses to this question determined whether they met the criteria as participants in this research and how they would answer subsequent Part B of the Interview Guide. Part A of the Interview Guide explores how self-leadership supports team building. Part B of the Interview Guide explores the barriers to self-leadership in team building. Eighteen of the 20 participants answered yes to the first research question. All questions in Part A of the Interview Guide followed the same format. Two participants answered no to the first research question before proceeding to Part B of the Interview Guide, the RQ 2.

All interview questions in Part A of the guide were designed to address the analysis's Research Question 1 (RQ1). Research question RQ1 explores how self-leadership supports team building in an organization and considers the barriers to leaders' team-building ability. In Part A, questions 1 through 7, inquiries were made regarding establishing a leadership development training, self-leadership curriculum, the value the training brings to the organization's success, and initial perceptions and views. Questions following the opening question were inquisitive and prompting questions. These questions were generated to produce spontaneous, exhaustive, and expressive responses from the participants. This action allowed the participants to reflect upon individual experiences and emotional states while creating data that allowed for new themes and concepts.

This research study's first developing theme resulted from the answers to the first question in Part A of the Interview Guide and the follow-up questions. The theme that emerged from interview questions 1 through 7 was based on the participant's preference for adopting self-leadership in the leadership development program's curriculum. Seventeen of the 20 participants answered yes to question 1D, that self-leadership should be part of the leadership Development Program curriculum. All twenty participants answered yes to question 7, "would you recommend to emerging leaders the adoption of the concept of self-leadership in your current organization?" Subsequent questions following the opening question resulted in the first developing theme of the participants' preference for leadership competency. These are leadership skills and behaviors that contribute to superior performance.

Increased self-leadership skills will improve a leader's self-management behavior (Lee, Park, and Choi (2020).

Self-leadership Training Supports Leadership Competency. The participants agree that self-leadership training leads to leadership competency and self-leadership in the leadership development program curriculum. Mentorship aided self-leadership among the team, and 11 of the 20 participants had mentors. Ten of the participants believed their mentors supported them in becoming better self-leaders. One of the respondents said their mentor influenced and inspired them to reach their goals through constant communication. Nine of the participants indicated their mentors did intellectually challenge them with new perspectives and ideas.

The following three developing themes address the research question RQ1. These themes appeared from questions 1 through 7 of the Interview Guide and additional questions. The next theme highlights the importance of self-leadership and how their organization should mandate leadership training. Seventeen participants said their organizations do not require self-leadership training. Eleven participants agreed that their organizations should make self-leadership training a requirement for anyone appointed to a leadership role.

The themes address Part B's research questions, which is RQ2. The eighth question is on how the participants would characterize the concept of self-leadership in the organization. Ntshingila, Downing, and Hastings-Tolsma (2021) suggest that the idea of self-leadership requires an individual to control personal actions, be self-aware, and utilize personal strength to perform tasks effectively. The ninth question was whether the participants had the opportunity to participate in any leadership development program before promotion to a leadership position. According to Sánchez (2020), improving a leader's self-leadership training involves diverse organizational perspectives. The tenth question was whether the participants considered seeking out self-leadership training in the new leadership role. The eleventh question discussed what the participants consider the benefits of having self-leadership training for their team members.

The twelfth question was for the participants to describe their perceptions and views on establishing self-leadership training. Martha Pitta Uli Marpaung, Suza, and Arruum (2019) emphasized that self-leadership training is vital to organizational work behavior. Kalra, Agnihotri, Singh, Puri, and Kumar (2020) suggest that self-efficacy is positively related to behavioral self-leadership, which relates to adaptive performance. The thirteenth question discussed whether the participants believe self-leadership would have aided them in their current leadership position. The fourteenth question asked whether the participants believed that the influence of self-leadership would have benefited the organization and overall business. The fifteenth question asked if the participants believe self-leadership would help build credibility, trust, and authenticity as a leader. The sixteenth and final question asked whether the participants could create a plan and schedule and not lose focus on a set goal.

These themes contribute to the body of knowledge on how self-leadership influences team building and barriers to leaders' team-building ability. The answers provided by participants show there are individual and organizational barriers to team building. Participants agreed that to overcome any self-leadership obstacle in their organization, learning and self-development, improved people skills, and self-regulation are critical factors for success. Self-regulation involves controlling one's behavior, emotions, and thoughts to pursue long-term goals. More specifically, emotional self-regulation refers to the ability to manage disruptive emotions and impulses (Cuncic, 2020). Fifteen respondents said they had the opportunity to participate in leadership development programs sponsored by the organization to develop and improve their people skills before being promoted to a leadership position. Nine respondents consider seeking out self-leadership training in their new leadership role.

Seventeen respondents agreed that self-leadership training would have aided them in their leadership position. Seventeen of the 20 participants believe that self-leadership influence would have aided their organization and overall business success. Eighteen of the 20 respondents believe that self-leadership would help them build credibility, trust, and authenticity as a leader. Sixteen of the 20 respondents mentioned that they could create a plan and schedule and not lose focus on a set goal which is the attribute of self-leadership.

Training and development help organizations gain and retain top talent, increase employees' job satisfaction, build morale, and improve productivity for overall success. Five of the respondents are in senior leadership positions, and they apply all the characteristics of self-leaders. The skills they have acquired have enabled them to build a cohesive team in their respective business unit. The respondents' views on establishing self-leadership training are divided into perceived value, a proposed design, and the perception that makes self-leadership a mandatory requirement that will support building a cohesive team. In the final analysis, we considered the benefits of self-leadership training and how it supports team-building. The ability to focus on critical factors such as team efficacy and enhanced knowledge and skills will help improve a leader's propensity to succeed.

CHAPTER 9

SELF-LEADERSHIP STRATEGY

Learning Objectives:

- Constructive thought strategies
- Behavior-focused strategies
- Natural reward strategies
- Team building interventions
- Team-building activities

Self-leadership is a recent concept suggested in leadership and is based on the notion that people should first lead themselves before leading others (Uzman & Maya, 2019). Self-leadership consists of several strategies such as behavioral focus, constructive thought, and natural reward (Uzman & Maya, 2019). Leaders use these cognitive, behavioral, and emotional strategies to control their behaviors, influence themselves, and lead themselves (Uzman & Maya, 2019). A recent research study applied a gender-aware framework to examine the self-leadership strategies that men and women in early-stage high-growth entrepreneurs employ to develop innovations (Bendell, Sullivan, & Marvel, 2018). Male entrepreneurs who use more robust goal-setting behaviors increase intellectual property development than females (Bendell et al., 2018).

Behavior-focused strategies. Behavior-focused strategies result in an individual's focus on his behaviors, thus making modifications to his behaviors. Self-punishment controls undesirable behaviors. Self-goal-setting strategies create accurate long-term and short-term goals (Uzman & Maya, 2019). Individuals can set challenging and specific goals more effectively to increase individual performance levels significantly (Pavlovic, 2019). Self-rewards may be something simple or intangible such as mentally congratulating oneself for a critical accomplishment, or something more concrete, like a unique vacation after a complex project (Pavlovic, 2019). Self-punishment or self-correcting feedback should consist of a positively framed and introspective examination of failures and undesirable behaviors leading to reshaping such behaviors (Bum, 2018). This type of self-awareness is a necessary first step toward changing or eliminating ineffective and unproductive behaviors (Bum, 2018).

Constructive thought strategies. These are composed of imagining, self-talk, and evaluating beliefs and assumptions (Uzman & Maya, 2019). Constructive thought strategies focus on an individual's thoughts, and they involve the re-regulation of those thoughts according to whether they are healthy (Uzman & Maya, 2019). Constructive thought pattern strategies include identifying and replacing dysfunctional beliefs and assumptions, mental imagery, and positive self-talk (Pavlovic, 2019). Individuals should first examine their thought patterns and confront dysfunctional, irrational beliefs and assumptions with more constructive thought processes (Pavlovic, 2019). Self-talk is what people covertly tell themselves, and it involves mental self-evaluations and reactions (Bum, 2018). Behavior-focused self-leadership strategies encourage positive and desirable behaviors that lead to successful outcomes (Bum, 2018).

Natural reward strategies. Natural reward strategies are emotional strategies that highlight the enjoyable and satisfying aspects of a job or a task and ignore the unpleasant (Uzman & Maya, 2019). Another study suggested that the natural reward strategies influence leader's initial emotion-regulating abilities, while leadership skills partially mediate in the natural reward strategies–performance relationship (Singh, Singh, & Banerji, 2018). Several theories synthesize, develop, and test the impact of emotional regulation on natural reward strategies components of self-leadership among leaders (Singh, Singh, & Banerji, 2018). Subsequently, direct effects on performance have a mediating impact on leadership skills (Bum, 2018). There are two types of natural rewards: the reward received by the leader who leaves an organization after the service completion; the other is the reward received by the leader who leaves the organization due to fallout or personal issues (Gao, Niu, & Li, 2017). Study shows that self-leadership strategies positively affect individuals' lives (Uzman & Maya, 2019).

Team Building Intervention

Team Building Intervention is the thematic focus of this research. Team building is a process intervention prompting team members to reflect on their behavior (Jones, Napiersky & Lyubovnikova, 2019). Learning and development needs have shifted from a sole focus on individual development in the context of its functions to enhancing team effectiveness (Jones, Napiersky, & Lyubovnikova, 2019). Team building's group-based intervention fosters group cohesion and exercises adherence (Forrest & Bruner, 2017). Team building interventions have typically used a leader present within the exercise set to deliver the intervention, and team building is beneficial to the organization (Forrest & Bruner, 2017).

There is diversity in the literature regarding how to label team-building approaches themselves, with some authors using the term team-building intervention (Miller, Kim, Silverman, & Bauer, 2018). Positive findings regarding the utility of team-building interventions temper a lack of control conditions, inconsistency in outcome measures, and a high probability of bias (Miller, Kim, Silverman, & Bauer, 2018). Considering well-recognized teamwork could develop evidence-based team building (Miller, Kim, Silverman, & Bauer, 2018). Team building's group-based intervention fosters group cohesion and exercises adherence (Forrest & Bruner, 2017). Team building interventions have typically used a leader present within the exercise location to deliver the intervention (Forrest & Bruner, 2017). For instance, team building protocol tailors an online delivery method that utilizes many social media tools to benefit team building. It is crucial to allow leaders to develop their strategies because various leaders have different personalities and methods of implementation (Forrest & Bruner, 2017).

Team-building activities. Team members need to perform well on a task function by working together for the team to succeed. The relationships between team-related factors and team effectiveness, team performance, or team outputs are present in several team effectiveness models (Fung, 2018). Team-building activities such as the commercial escape rooms and others utilize effective team-building activities by immersing participants in interactive and unpredictable activities (Zhang, Lee, Rodriguez, Rudner, Chan, & Dimitrios, 2018). This activity allows learners to immerse themselves in an engaging, fun, non-threatening, non-clinical, low-stakes activity that rewards teamwork and effective leadership, resulting in employee satisfaction (Zhang et al., 2018). Employee satisfaction with their team-building activities provides feedback to improve the future experience, resulting in teamwork (Ireland, Deloney, Renfroe, & Jambhekar, 2017).

Team-building activities provide employees the feeling that belonging to their workgroup is extremely important (Ireland et al., 2017). The reason is that family, friendships, and social connections are essential to being happy even in the work environment (Ireland et al., 2017). Team building provides employees opportunities to satisfy these needs early in the transition process (Ireland et al., 2017). Teams perform team-building activities that promote either team or task outcomes and deploy team-building activities to foster interpersonal relations (Hastings, Jahanbakhsh, Karahalios, Marinov, & Bailey, 2018). Leaders deploy a team formation tool and create expectations among team members to perform well with teams in various criteria (Hastings et al., 2018). The criteria-based teams did not statistically differ from the random teams on any of the measures taken, despite having compositions that better satisfied the criteria defined by the leader (Hastings et al., 2018).

Teamwork. Team members should effectively overcome varying training and expertise levels, conflicting personalities, and diverse skill sets to function as a unit (Zhang et al., 2018). Studies demonstrate that effective teamwork and collaboration, particularly in high-stake environments, are beneficial to the employees due to effective leadership (Zhang et al., 2018). However, ineffective leadership contributes to poor team coordination, inefficiency, and adverse outcomes, while effective team coordination and success during these critical initial interventions are essential for optimal results (Grimsley, Cochrane, Keane, Sumner, Mullan, & O'Connell, 2019). The question arises as to whether the quest to make everyone a leader and convince them to take on a leadership role to communicate reasonably, is consistent with the desire for interprofessional teamwork (Mainous, 2018).

In an organization, teams need to understand and commit to the concepts of open communication, situational awareness, and continuous learning (Keats, 2019). The way to improve teamwork is mainly by changing organizational culture (Thomas, Lal, Mishra, Thapa, & Mosser, 2019). Effective team collaboration is crucial in today's complex system (Thomas et al., 2019). A wide range of studies has shown the positive effects of teamwork interventions for improving team effectiveness across several contexts (McEwan, Ruissen, Eys, Zumbo, & Beauchamp, 2017). There are positive and significantly low effects of teamwork interventions on team performance and improved teamwork training (McEwan et al., 2017). The teamwork improvements result from training with various team types, including new teams (McEwan et al., 2017). Teamwork involves the execution of core technical competencies within a given domain; teamwork refers to the range of interactive and interdependent behavioral processes among team members that convert team inputs (McEwan et al., 2017).

Communication. Communication and teamwork enable the ability to communicate information, ideas, problems, and solutions with organizations and professionals effectively and significantly, and to function effectively in a local, national or international context, as an individual, and as a team member by collaborating effectively (Malheiro, Guedes, Silva, & Ferreira, 2019). Effective communication is the starting point for building trust. Effective communication plays a vital role in building and maintaining long-term relationships (Kharouf, Sekhon, Fazal-e-Hasan, Hickman, & Mortimer, 2019). Communication is essential in building trust due to collecting and accumulating evidence about the organization's integrity, benevolence, and competence (Kharouf et al., 2019). Furthermore, effective communication and trust impact behavioral and attitudinal loyalty (Kharouf et al., 2019). This notion supports the study suggesting that self-leadership and communication competence positively correlated with performance (Yu & Ko, 2017).

Communication competency plays a partial mediating role in the relationship between self-leadership and job performance (Yu & Ko, 2017). Communication competency, self-leadership, and personal factors are critical factors influencing organizational performance (Yu & Ko, 2017). Communication competency is likely to vary among members of the same organization. There is a significantly positive correlation between self-leadership and job performance, making it necessary to reinforce self-leadership and successfully respond to organizational environments' changes that maximize job performance (Yu & Ko, 2017). Leaders should have the required skills and strategies to develop communicative competence and improve self-leadership recognition to achieve high performance (Yu & Ko, 2017).

Self-leadership constructs. This qualitative case study research study explores the concept of self-leadership importance in team building. For this study, self-leadership is an intrinsic motivation to influence self-regarding what, why, and how to perform work (Rambe, Modise, & Chipunza, 2018). This study explores the relationship between the independent constructs and the dependent constructs of self-leadership and team building. According to Mulder (2019), some personal attributes are necessary to foster learning from experiences to develop leadership potential. Mulder (2019) asserts that the primary variable that influences experiential learning is the capacity and practice of self-reflection.

Mulder (2019) believes that drawing lessons from experiences drive leadership development, and self-reflection increases the number of tasks noticed in each experience. Mulder (2019) emphasized that leaders' inexperience is challenging and don't promote learning. Zaech and Baldegger (2017) describe leadership as an interaction between two or more group members that often involves structuring or restructuring the situation, perceptions, and expectations. Zaech and Baldegger (2017) emphasized that self-leadership can impact the effectiveness of leadership behavior. Zaech and Baldegger (2017) believe that leaders appeal to their followers' self-interest to motivate them to achieve specific tasks.

In self-leadership, authenticity is an attribute of effective leaders, just as trust is the basis of every relationship (Parker, 2017). Authenticity allows a leader to show imperfection and an element of humanity that generates trust (Parker, 2017). This claim means that an authentic leader's integrity is never in question. Hence, a leader that desires to be more authentic could start with knowing themselves, which is the concept of self-awareness. Credibility focuses on the role of leaders and their ability to coordinate followers' actions through credibility. Kunißen (2019) suggests that many empirical studies dealing with these outcomes implement a multilevel design in the concept of credibility.

Drakeley (2018) believes in a relationship between followers' perceptions of self-leadership support and authenticity in leadership. Drakeley (2018) suggests that a leadership style can motivate and influence followers who lack hope, self-efficacy, and optimism and improve their commitment to the organization by providing a purpose in work and improving productivity. Drakeley (2018) emphasized that leadership studies differ widely in the design and constructs explored on a general level. Drakeley (2018) suggests that a leader's self-regulation, which produces an ethical environment, replaces the independent constructs to be notable regarding leadership behaviors and follower outcomes. Authenticity and credibility explore the relationship between other concepts discussed in this section.

A leader that desires to be more authentic could start with knowing themself, which is the concept of self-awareness.

According to Peragine and Hudgins (2017), trust is a significant factor that teammates should experience for their success. Peragine and Hudgins (2017) suggested that a team leader must build loyalty, choose individuals who fit, and work with other team members to portray effective leadership. Magpili-Smith (2017) suggests that lack of team trust is one factor that can inhibit the information elaboration process in teams because of the social-categorization process. Magpili-Smith (2017) concluded that teams with long-term relationships usually form trust based on past working experiences. Teamwork can enable the team members to have a higher level of emotional security, self-confidence, and the ability to positively plan and decide with others (Sanyal & Hisam, 2018).

This study suggests that teamwork helps develop employees' skills and perspectives by exchanging positive opinions, feedback, experiences, and viewpoints (Sanyal & Hisam, 2018). Trust in management mediates the relationship between different types of leadership and acceptance of change; transformational leadership is more effective in increasing both trust and acceptance of the change (Cai, Loon, & Wong, 2018). Trustworthiness is an important concept to foster trust through loyalty and leadership (Lesinger, Altinay, Altinay, Dagli, 2018). The leadership role is a moderating group dynamic and facilitates collaborative management for concerted learning (Lesinger et al., 2018). Professional development is successful through a strong network and interaction concerning trust and loyalty (Lesinger et al., 2018). The dependent construct includes trust and teamwork (Xu & Montague, 2019). This research explores the significant relationship between any one of the self-leadership concepts discussed.

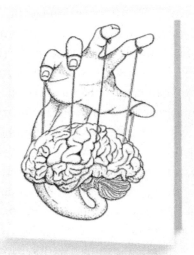

- Self-regulation – "the ability to monitor and manage one's thinking, attention, feelings, and behavior to accomplish goals." (Thompson, 2009)

CHAPTER 10

APPLICATION OF SELF-LEADERSHIP

Learning Objectives:

- The role of self-leadership in organizational development.
- Understand how to apply your self-leadership skills
- Identify various self-leadership patterns
- The significance of self-leadership training

Self-leadership remains a valid concept, and its understanding and application are likely to differ across cultures (Alves et al., 2006). Self-leadership enhances self-awareness, self-confidence, and good governance since the practice of intentionally influencing others by encouraging, motivating, guiding, and inspiring will change organizational thinking towards a positive path (Daud, 2020). The research conducted by Daud (2020) shows that self-leadership is an indispensable practice that can enable leaders in the contemporary business environment to manage change in the most efficient, effective, and sustainable way. Like any other organization, the governments deal with ineffective leaders among its ranks. To solve the problem of inefficient leadership, an organization must encourage self-leadership within its ranks. According to Cranmer, Goldman, and Houghton (2019), self-leadership processes influence organizational outcomes. Cranmer, Goldman, and Houghton, 2019) assert that self-leadership influences corporate leaders' adjustment and subsequent commitment by assisting them in seeking organizational resources. The above statement means that self-leadership is a critical skill required for leaders to be effective in building a cohesive team. Flores, Jiang, and Manz (2018) believe that leaders can avoid the negative effect of conflict in the workplace due to poor quality team decision-making.

The role of self-leadership in team building. Organizational stakeholders should enhance leaders' self-leadership abilities to build a cohesive team (Cranmer, Goldman, & Houghton, 2019). Lack of self-leadership makes it difficult for leaders to lead effectively (Müller & Niessen, 2019). Self-leadership plays a crucial role in leading or building a team (Müller & Niessen, 2019). Self-leadership is the key to understanding why cognitive conflict sometimes leads to improved decision quality (Flores, Jiang, & Manz, 2018). This idea supports the assertion that, through self-leadership, team members can actively anticipate, guide, and focus their emotional responses to cognitive conflict and reduce their experience of affective conflict, improving team decision quality (Flores, Jiang, & Manz, 2018). The self-leadership strategy serves as a mediating self-regulatory mechanism of leaders' differences in predicting individual creativity because it is related to actions intended to lead their goal-directed activities (Lin, 2017).

This qualitative case study's research questions addressed self-leadership role in influencing team building and barriers to team-building ability, lack of credibility, trust, and authenticity of leaders within an organization resulting in inefficient leadership. According to Marques (2017), self-leadership has risen to prominence in recent years due to the increased awareness of its importance for leaders in making more responsible decisions. The research questions also addressed the inclusion of self-leadership training in the Leadership Development Program curriculum. The research questions discussed further the benefit of a leadership development program and self-leadership training. The research questions also answered the question of whether self-leadership training should be a requirement in the organization. Goldsby, Goldsby, Neck, and Neck (2020) suggest that self-leadership can be an appropriate training tool for leaders to perform their roles as decision-makers.

Goldsby et al. (2020) ascertain that self-leadership can help leaders manage their thoughts, behaviors, and environment to create a better workplace for improved results. Goldsby et al. (2020) define self-leadership as the process in which people can regulate what they do, interact with others, and decide to lead themselves. Marques (2017) agrees that self-leadership is a self-influence process in which one leads, motivates, and controls personal behavior toward reaching self-defined goals. The questions further explored the leadership style that participants applied toward their team members, which encourages mentorship. The research questions additionally assessed if mentorship influenced or inspired the participant to reach their self-leadership goal. The relationship between self-leadership qualities and willingness to mentor can be explained by the improved sense of security and control among self-leaders (Ganesh, M Ángeles, & Vázquez-Rodríguez, 2019).

Several self-leadership theories and strategies were discussed in the literature review. In self-leadership research, studies have found empirical evidence that people engaging in self-leadership strategies are more likely to improve their task performance than people who are not utilizing self-leadership strategies (Lin, 2017). Self-leadership strategies are self-influencing processes through which leaders achieve the self-direction and self-motivation necessary to perform effectively (Lin, 2017). The influence of an individual's self-leadership is straightforward, which enhances creative performance (Lin, 2017). The self-leadership theory stresses the importance of creating and maintaining constructive thought patterns (Goldsby, Goldsby, & Neck, 2020). This research reinforces the notion that self-leadership cognitive strategies place responsibility for these thought patterns on the individual (Goldsby, Goldsby, & Neck, 2020). These thought patterns impact our perceptions, how we process information, and the choices we make almost automatically (Goldsby, Goldsby, & Neck, 2020).

Self-Leadership Thinking Pattern. There are two common and contrasting thinking patterns: opportunity and obstacle thinking (Goldsby, Goldsby, & Neck, 2020). An opportunity thinker focuses on constructive ways of dealing with challenges. In contrast, an obstacle thinker focuses on reasons to withdraw and retreat from problems (Goldsby, Goldsby, & Neck, 2020). A leader starting with a self-defeat attitude lessens their commitment to building a cohesive team, affecting future engagement with the entire team (Goldsby, Goldsby, & Neck, 2020). Team building interventions incorporate activities that focus on building self-efficacy, resilience, hope, and optimism (Harunavamwe, Pillay, & Nel, 2020). Self-efficacy mediates the effects of constructive thought patterns and self-leadership strategies (Harunavamwe, Pillay, & Nel, 2020). Self-leadership affects an individual's ability to connect with other people, teams, or groups in the organization (Harunavamwe, Pillay, & Nel, 2020).

The themes developed from this study are relevant to improving leadership competence and team-building ability through self-leadership training requirements for organizations. The interpersonal competencies and good relationships resulting from employee self-leadership training are directly linked to team effectiveness and higher workplace productivity (Gaur, 2019). There is a need to have different approaches toward your team based on their interpersonal desires to enhance their interpersonal and communication skills (Gaur, 2019). In the corporate world, individuals are encouraged to work as teams, and how well they maintain their interpersonal relations has become the indication of their overall success (Gaur, 2019). Na-Nan and Saribut (2020) describe self-leadership as a process in which people control their behavior and create influence through strategy and perception. Na-Nan and Saribut (2020) emphasized that self-leadership specifies a collection of intra-individual strategies that provide an explicit behavioral and cognitive prescription.

Another theme developed is self-leadership which identifies a leader's strengths and weaknesses. Self-leadership allows a person to identify their strong point and shortfalls. Self-monitoring positively moderates the relationship between thought self-leadership and adaptive behavior (Alnakhli, Singh, Agnihotri, & Itani, 2020). The self-monitoring mechanism directly affects a critical component of a business process and adaptive behavior (Alnakhli, Singh, Agnihotri, & Itani, 2020). Self-leadership strategies and self-monitoring are vital cognitive processes that drive adaptive behaviors (Alnakhli, Singh, Agnihotri, & Itani, 2020). Additionally, constructive thought strategies play a positive role in an individual's self-leading capabilities (Alnakhli,

Singh, Agnihotri, & Itani, 2020). Self-leadership is a process that can translate into the capability of handling challenges and sustaining self and others (Pina e Cunha, Pacheco, Castanheira, & Rego, 2017).

Organizations are now globally dependent on effective management and team building to be successful (Khan & Wajidi, 2019). The role of leadership is vital in building a cohesive team (Khan & Wajidi, 2019). The working environment and relationship between the leader and team members are key factors that create motivation and accelerate work to achieve goals (Khan & Wajidi, 2019). Team building functions are vital for group expertise and communication. Most organizations' success depends on the talent the leaders and team bring to build a cohesive team environment (Khan & Wajidi, 2019). In team development, it is imperative to identify the processes that fulfill the team's socio-emotional functions and between team members (Turunen & Hiltunen, 2019). Like trust and cohesion, the socio-emotional processes are necessary for building relationships within teams (Turunen & Hiltunen, 2019). Self-leadership quality gives a leader the credibility and trust to build a cohesive team. There is a need for mutual support and respect among the team members in team building (Turunen & Hiltunen, 2019).

Team building refers to the activities that improve a team's effectiveness by developing working relationships, better understanding, alignment among members, enhanced communications, and trust (Misra & Srivastava, 2018). Team building is the process of helping a group of individuals, bound by a shared sense of purpose, to work interdependently with each other, the leader, external stakeholders, and the organization (Fung, 2018). Effective teams are not a matter of luck; they are the outcomes of hard work, careful planning, and good training (Flaming & Mosca, 2019). Team members who feel comfortable with each other have a higher level of trust (Flaming & Mosca, 2019). Leadership is less about one person's authority and more about the team's collective success (Flaming & Mosca, 2019). Leadership relates to having a stronger relationship between individual task performance and team performance (Misra & Srivastava, 2018).

The team's effective formation requires that the leader have the relevant skills, strategic thinking, psychological culture, and the ability to assess the professional competence of candidates' social and personal qualities (Grynchenko, Ponomaryov, & Lobach, 2018). A leader's capability to foster the team members' professional and personal development is valuable (Grynchenko, Ponomaryov, & Lobach, 2018). A leader should use a transparent process of motivation and incentives to build and organize teamwork (Grynchenko, Ponomaryov, & Lobach, 2018). Team building consists of all activities to improve team members' problem-solving ability by resolving task and interpersonal issues that hamper the team's functionality (Fung, 2018). Organizational leaders encourage team-building efforts to resolve conflicts within the team to maintain team performance (Fung, 2018). Teams are formed to achieve corporate objectives as organizations generally recognize the importance and benefits of project teams (Fung, 2018).

Teamwork is positively associated with perceived employee job satisfaction (Kopina, 2019). The level of self-management is positively associated with the perceived team performance (Kopina, 2019). There is a significant and positive correlation between teamwork and job satisfaction (Kopina, 2019). Shared leadership will often not be successful when individual team members have different or inconsistent understandings of their goals and priorities (Pretorius, Steyn, & Bond-Barnard, 2017). Teamwork goals may suffer from absent or weak shared leadership, which could erode trust in the leader (Pretorius, Steyn, & Bond-Barnard, 2017). Trust affects team performance by initiating teamwork and other collaborative processes that make the team successful (Pretorius, Steyn, & Bond-Barnard, 2017). Trusting teams can naturally manage the interdependencies among their diverse areas of expertise better (Pretorius, Steyn, & Bond-Barnard, 2017).

Recommendations for Action

This study focused on exploring the influence of self-leadership in team building and the barriers that hinder team building within an organization to address the lack of self-leadership resulting in leaders' inability to build a cohesive team. The themes developed during the field study analysis include the preference for developing leadership competency, human skills, self-leadership training, professional skill, self-development, team orientation, and specific learning and growth. The themes identified during the analysis of the interview in the participants' field study produced three recommended actions. These recommendations support the guarantee that businesses and organizational leaders determine the significance of self-leadership training in leaders' team-building abilities. These recommendations include developing a self-leadership training curriculum in all phases of the leadership development program, requiring every candidate for the position of a supervisor to take self-leadership training, and using the LDP to develop a supervisory career pathway to apply learned skills in the LDP program.

Develop a self-leadership training curriculum. One of the themes referenced from the field study interview process was establishing a self-leadership training curriculum in all leadership development programs, focusing on team-building abilities. Including self-leadership training in the LDP will enable future leaders and supervisors to have the necessary skill for leading others. Leaders must first learn to lead themselves before having the capacity to lead others in the organization. Self-leadership training should be made available even outside the leadership development program for individuals who aspire to be in a leadership position. Equipping oneself with self-leadership skills will always be valuable for effective leadership.

Require self-leadership training for supervisors. The key to business success is having leaders with practical decision-making skills and the ability to influence themselves to work effectively and independently. Self-leadership enables leaders to build stronger team relationships, and become more self-aware and disciplined. Requiring or encouraging supervisors to take self-leadership training will be a value-added to organizational success. Self-leadership will allow a leader to influence others to act on vital issues to achieve the organization's goals. Additionally, self-leadership will aid the leader in achieving their individual and professional goals. Self-leadership values include making a leader more efficient and productive and helping the leader remain motivated to motivate others and be more accountable to the team and the entire organization.

Establish a supervisory career path for applying learned skills in the LDP. Applying the recently learned self-leadership skill from the leadership development program is the most critical ability any emerging leader can display if given the opportunity. The ability to showcase what an individual learned from the LDP is the most rewarding experience the organization can provide. Failure to apply learned skills is a waste of the individual's time and organizational resources. Creating a supervisory career path will reward individuals who are nominated to participate in the leadership development program. One of the best ways to help employees appreciate what they learned is to have them apply in a new way or practical sense what they have learned from the leadership development program. Escudier, Woolford, and Tricio (2018) suggest applying theoretical knowledge to specific problem-solving is the most critical and valuable use of what is learned. Organizations can influence how individuals' learned knowledge is applied to a leadership development program (Kersten, Taminiau, Schuurman, Weggeman, & Embregts, 2018).

> *Trust affects team performance by initiating teamwork and other collaborative processes that make the team successful (Pretorius et al., 2017).*

Implementation of recommendations. There are three key recommendations that organizational leaders should adopt in self-leadership. These recommendations are also significant in a leader's team-building abilities. Additionally, the successful implementation of these recommendations could be achieved if championed by the Chief Strategy Officer and the Human Capital Management Office. First, all recommendations must be encouraged by the decision-makers and senior leadership of the organization. It is critical to get the senior executive's buy-in because when senior leaders recognize and support recommendations, their application becomes more generally accepted and effectively implemented (Guttenberg, 2020). Second, the human capital management office must include self-leadership training in the leadership development program curriculum; make self-leadership a required skill in the process of hiring supervisors.

The office of the Chief Strategy Officer must develop a strategy for including the supervisory career path in the Leadership Development Program and making the program rewarding by placing LDP alumni on a promotional path once they graduate from the program. The Chief Strategy Office and the Human Capital Management Office should develop a strategic framework for applying learned skills from any organization-sponsored training program. This action will help them share what they have learned from the leadership development program. The organization must establish a mechanism for measuring the value of training provided to the workforce. There should be a strategy for measuring the benefits of self-leadership training to the organization, the importance of any leadership, and how individuals can apply the skills learned from leadership development program training. There should be a practical feedback mechanism provided. The organization must implement participants' feedback in the Leadership Development Program or any organization's executive training.

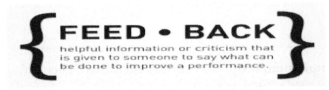

Image adapted from emPerform

CHAPTER 11

RELATIONAL LEADERSHIP

Learning Objectives:

- Understand the concept of relational leadership

- Understand the importance of relational leadership

- Understand the role of leadership in an organization

Relational leadership is purposeful, inclusive, empowering, and ethical (Ramamoorthi et al., 2021). Multiple theoretical frameworks that combine relational leadership and leadership trichotomy were adapted to study factors that enable shared and relational practices (Ramamoorthi et al., 2021). Teams can actively build collaboration in learning spaces through manifesting relational leadership (Ramamoorthi et al., 2021). Effective leaders must develop and build a stronger relationship with the people they inspire to follow them. Effective leaders inspire people through relationships to become more than they imagined they could become and achieve more for the benefit of everyone—small and large gestures of friendship nurture authentic and empathetic relational leadership. Effective leaders who have credible, trusting, and authentic relationships with their teams understand the importance of investing time and effort in building these bonds. Great leaders know that leadership is a relationship, and leaders with toxic relationships with their teams will have poor performance. Mastering personal relationships that build trust and create a collaborative work environment is central to leadership effectiveness (Ready, 2019). Relational leaders must have a genuine concern for the growth and development of others.

President George H.W. Bush applied the relational approach to leadership with values and personality. Relational leadership helps build alliances and partnerships. Relational leadership is grounded on empathy by understanding people and coming to the same level as them. In 1989, when the Berlin Wall fell, President Bush was criticized for his submissive response. People would have preferred that the president celebrate more publicly. In politics, relationships among lawmakers and community members often lead to compromise, while trust is an essential component of business partnership. However, President Bush understood how tense a political moment the event was for Soviet General Secretary Mikhail Gorbachev, and sensitive to his relationship with Gorbachev and the fragility of the moment, the American president avoided rejoicing not to worsen the situation.

Relational leadership is about trust, and to be in any relationship, you must trust that individual. Establish a trusting relationship by having a regular discussion with a team member to share a mutual understanding of your respective expectations, drives, motivations, and preferences for productivity and accountability, resulting in high performance at work. Relationships are essential enablers of a leader's ability to attract, keep and get the very best out of their team members and colleagues. A relational leader is authentic in appreciating the collaborative relationship with the team. The relationship helps the team members focus on their successes, and the relational leader helps the team understand that collaboration is the reason for their success. Great leaders understand that personal relationships build trust and create a collaborative work environment.

Relational leadership matters to countries. For instance, Americans are frequently told of the importance of building a stronger relationship with their "allies," but what does it mean to be a United States ally? These relationships are considered critical to American security but frequently contentious. Additionally, America's strong leadership in the world today centers on its relationship with its Allies. Remembering the tragedy of September 11, 2001, the terrorists attacked the United States. America went to war along with its allies. Also, when allies are involved, the question of how to generate "fair" burden-sharing provisions becomes a challenge in U.S. alliances.

However, the United States has gained enormous benefits from these relationships in the protection of the homeland. The theory behind establishing the U.S. alliance system was that building the capabilities of like-minded states and creating a network of collective defense measures would effectively and efficiently protect America's global interests. For more than seven decades, America's alliances in Asia and Europe have promoted democracy, market economies, the rule of law, and respect for human rights. While the formal defense requirements of U.S. treaty alliances are relatively small, there are significant security benefits from these relationships. Constantly, the U.S. and its allies share intelligence, train, and exercise and create combined capabilities that far exceed any force the U.S. could wield alone.

Relationships are essential enablers of a leader's ability to attract, keep and get the very best out of their team members and colleagues.

Leadership is about solving the problems of others. Relational leadership is about using empathy and care to solve those problems. General Collin Power, former U.S. Secretary of State, said, "Leadership is solving problems. The day soldiers stop bringing you their problems is the day you have stopped leading them. They have either lost confidence that you can help or conclude you do not care. Either case is a failure of leadership." No one will take their problems to someone unless they trust and have confidence that the person can solve the problem. It is vital to have a real connection with the team members. The millennial workforce wants an authentic and genuine relationship with their team members in the workplace. People want to know you care about their needs and that the leader sees them as valuable team members. Leaders must take time to learn about the families and lives of the teams outside of work. When someone doesn't meet your expectations, discuss with them and make it known as a leader. Ask what happened and be ready to listen to them to understand their perspectives without judging. Explain why their performance matters to you, the team, and the organization. I believe when you care about their challenges, they will care about the outcome and organization.

The TEAM LEAD Model shows that a relational leader will lead the team to learn by encouraging self-motivation. The team lead model shows that training helps the leader develop and become competent through self-motivation. Daniel Pink's theory of motivation centers on mastery as a motivator. Mastery is a critical component of intrinsic motivation and is described as the desire to get better at something that matters. Today's workforce cares about learning, at least for their personal development, and organizational leaders must pay attention to that and leverage it to their advantage. Team members know that all they have when they quit a job is their skills, which is enough to secure them a new job. If a leader is unwilling to help them learn, they will abandon the job quicker than you know and take all the knowledge they have acquired to the next organization. A relational leader encourages their team members to accomplish the goal if they make up their mind. The leader must use team engagement, bonding time, and team-building activities to encourage the team by pointing out progress and celebrating the team's successes. Gallup's employee engagement research provides a more precise estimate of the influence of team engagement on performance outcomes than any one study can capture.

Image: Building relationship - adapted from Max International

Lastly, relational leaders are inclusive, and inclusive leaders value diversity of thoughts. They consider everyone's perspective and experiences when making decisions. A great leader will ultimately make critical decisions in the organization, but only after considering all perspectives. Relational leaders empower their team members. They identify their team member's strengths and weaknesses and work to build on strengths and improve weaknesses. A relational leader values the professional growth of the team. They can communicate a clear purpose because they are very active listeners. Relational leaders have an enterprising mindset, they begin with the end in mind, and their resourcefulness leads to achieving a common goal. Leadership is about relationships. Leaders will never be leaders without followers. People follow leaders because of authenticity, credibility, and trust by connecting and believing in the leaders' vision and voluntarily participating for mutual benefit created through relationships. America is great today because the citizens believe in its founding fathers' vision of a nation with the unalienable rights of life, liberty, and the pursuit of happiness. In times of crisis, Americans always come together, just as we witnessed on September 11, 2001, and during the recent covid-19 pandemic in 2020, where various scientists came together to tackle the pandemic. The traditional leadership theories emphasize the what and how, while relational leadership focuses on the who. Hence, there is an urgent need to apply the TEAM LEAD model through relational leadership to address the leadership gap.

Relational Leadership

" A leader is someone who sets aside a personal agenda and embraces a greater agenda of serving others. "

Flip Flippen

CHAPTER 12

LEADERSHIP BLINDSPORTS

Learning Objectives:

- Understand Leadership Blindspot

- Identify Various Leadership Blindspots

Managing people is hard work; it's not for timid people but for leaders who can identify their blind spots. On the flip side of any leader's blind spots is their strength. Leadership is not about pleasing people but about doing the right thing and taking bold steps. I will share my leadership experience as a manager. After graduating from one of the Major Oil Corporation's management trainee programs in 2004, my first assignment as a young manager was at Virginia. The Oil Corporation had a long history of leadership in the petroleum and chemical manufacturing industries. Its greatest strengths are its high-quality directors, officers, and employees, ingenuity, and long-term perspective. The great thing about this program is that the organization pairs you with other seasoned leaders to mentor you, and as soon you are done with the training school, you will be assigned a management position.

I was accompanied to my first location by a seasoned manager who mentored me to have real-life experience as a manager. When we arrived at the new site, my deputy was at the door to welcome us and for me to take leadership of the place. To put things into perspective, I have never met this individual, but I have heard of him– let's call him Mr. A. He's been employed there for a while, knows the processes, and has probably seen many managers come and go. As we approached the door, we saw Mr. A, and I introduced myself and my colleague to him. The first thing he said was, "Oh! Are you the guy that just graduated from the management trainee program? The blind leading the blind."

He said it with a smile, turned around, and walked towards my new office, and we followed. My colleague looked at me in shock, as if to say, "what in the world" but in a more surprising way. Frankly, I did not know how to respond to this guy. I was not expecting this type of comment from him because he was supposed to be the deputy, and we will be working together, trust each other and share ideas for the benefit of the organization.

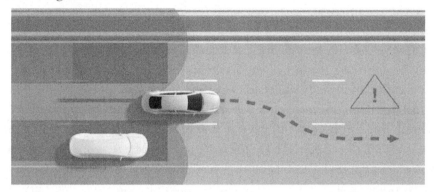

Another thing I experienced was that before I got there, I couldn't speculate why they all quit, but one thing I knew was that a change was needed. My first day was already challenging because of the wrong perception of my deputy about me. Several employees had quit, and I thought of the daunting task of hiring new employees, giving them orientation, and training them to be up to speed in doing their job. In week one, the first thing I did was meet with my direct supervisor to understand his expectations, share my objectives, and then meet with the remaining employees one on one before the first team meeting. No matter the type of manager or supervisor you are, managing people takes training, having an enterprising mindset, being authentic, being mindful, listening to employees, being empathetic, being accountable, and the ability to delegate authority. These are the core attributes of the TEAM LEAD model for effective Leadership.

> *Leadership is not about pleasing people but it is about doing the right thing and taking bold steps that might not be popular at that point in time.*

My experience as a leader in the Oil Corporation taught me that leadership is not about pleasing people but about doing the right thing and taking bold steps. I went through the preparation of the management trainee program to get the necessary skill to lead, but nothing prepared me for the comment of "blind leading blind" from my deputy. However, Mr. A's comment immediately reminded me that I have a blind spot as a leader, and it was my duty to identify those blind spots if I wanted to be a successful leader. As a leader, how do you identify your blind spots? More importantly, how do you fix the blind spots when you identify them? Leaders deal with people who judge them and have strong opinions about them without even knowing their capabilities. In my experience in Oil Corporation as a leader, I came into a management position after several months of management trainee school. Still, nothing could have prepared me to deal with people in a real-life experience, such as having a deputy like Mr. A, who already had a strong opinion about my ability to lead. Mr. A showed his displeasure by working against my vision and was willing to sabotage every effort and decision I made as a leader. Also, before transitioning to the government sector, I gained more competence and became a training manager/coach and eventually trained and mentored many managers in the corporation.

In the statement "the blind leading blind," if we get things into perspective, the question is, who is "the blind"? And who is the "leader" in this case? As a man of faith, the statement reminds me of the verse I came across in the scripture in Luke 6:39 (NLT) "Then Jesus gave the following illustration: "Can one blind person lead another? Won't they both fall into a ditch?" The meaning of this passage in the scripture is that incompetent leaders will hurt both themselves and those following them. You cannot give what you don't have because as the teacher is, so is the student. We see the same thing in the book of Matthew 15:14 (NLT) "so ignore them. They are blind guides leading the blind, and if one blind person guides another, they will both fall into a ditch." To be an effective guide to others, a leader must see where they are going. A blind leader and a blind follower will be a dangerous combination. Blind leaders surround themselves with "Yes People," who lack diversity of thoughts, have a know-it-all attitude, are self-centered, cannot take criticism, and have a mistaken perception of their authority. A blind leader is like a driver who refuses to pay attention to their blind spots on the highway; he will be lucky to make it to their destination alive.

In 2017, I was on Interstate 95 heading south and driving home after work. The traffic was heavy as usual; in fact, the average speed at that moment might have been between 10-20 miles per hour on a 60 miles per hour highway. I was on the far-left lane, the speed lane, and noticed a U-Haul truck in my rearview mirror in the middle lane. This truck was towing another smaller vehicle. Within minutes, the driver in the middle lane had moved a little bit ahead of me and was trying to come over to my lane. I immediately beeped my car horn to get their attention. I slowed down because the car they were towing was moving in a zigzag manner, but the driver kept trying to move over to my lane without paying attention.

Another problem was that the driver ignored their blind spot because they would have noticed that the front of my car was in their blind spot. In the end, it cost them and their insurance $1800 worth of damage. It is a sign of arrogance when leaders refuse to listen or pay attention to their followers when they identify their blind spots by constructively criticizing poor performance. An arrogant leader wants to meet his/her self-centered target which is problematic. Leaders must pay attention to what their followers are saying. I remember beeping my car horn before the accident but the other driver was not paying attention. I slowed down, but the driver's target and focus were only to come over to my lane which resulted in the damage.

Leadership blind spots. Leadership blind spots are the specific areas where a leader is lacking or missing something. The fact is that even a great leader could have blind spots. A blind spot can be a lack of attention to a specific area or a part of the leader's skill set that never really developed for them to be competent. Every leader has blind spots. According to Shaw (2014), blind spots are unrecognized weaknesses or threats that hinder a leader's success.

The weaknesses and threats we don't know about are dangerous and can make a leader ineffective. To be successful as a manager, I had to identify my leadership blind spot. In this case, Mr. A, my deputy, was my blind spot because I found out that he was hoarding knowledge and withholding critical information that I needed for seamless operations. It is essential to eliminate blind spots that will keep us from effectively leading our teams as leaders. There are several leadership blind spots, but I will share the most common one with my experience.

The first leadership blind spot is a paradigm shift of the leader's purpose. After a while, successful leaders begin to overlook the reason they became a leader. They forget the 'why' in the TEAM LEAD framework on page 6. Leaders forget that their goal could differ from the organization's goal or the team members' goal. It is essential to be on the same page with the team members and understand why a team member is still on your team and why they do what they do. A leader must know the purpose and why they are in the leadership position. To fix this blind spot, the leader must constantly solicit feedback from the team members. Always ask the team members to tell you what they see as your blind spot that you should know.

The most obvious way to help leaders identify their blind spots is to review lessons learned and look for frequent weaknesses. The most effective way to assess a situation is to create formal and informal feedback processes. To apply the TEAM LEAD model, the leader must be mindful of the team and the work environment, become more aware of the employees and the organization's mission and pay attention to the needs of the employees. As leaders receive feedback on their blind spots, they must approach a trusted person to hold them accountable for any paradigm shift in purpose and behavior.

The second leadership blind spot is a leader that surrounds themselves with "yes people." A leader needs to have diverse thinkers with the intention of learning from them. Even the leader's approach to learning should reflect various perspectives, experiences, strategies, and tactics to problem-solving that they can adapt to any challenging situation. These leaders surround themselves with people who tell them what they want to hear and protect themselves from conflicting data and perspectives. These leaders don't want their viewpoints challenged. According to Merriam-Webster, a "yes person" is one who endorses or supports without criticism every opinion or proposal of an associate or superior. Suppose a leader does not allow team members to disagree constructively about something happening in the workplace. In that case, their actions mean that they do not value the diverse opinion of their team. To apply the TEAM LEAD model, the leader must have an enterprising mindset to be resourceful by bringing in various ideas, skills, and experiences to help them become more objective in their decision-making.

An incompetent leader is bound to hurt the chances of them succeeding and that of their followers. The truth remain that you cannot give what you do not have as a leader.

The third leadership blind spot is when a leader is not authentic. We have established that authenticity makes the leader credible. When the team notices that the leader is not authentic, they will stop coming to them to share information to help solve problems. General Colin Powell famously said, "Leadership is solving problems. The day soldiers stop bringing you their problems is the day you have stopped leading them." An authentic leader will not actively avoid uncomfortable conversations with the people under their chain of command. Everyone deserves candid conversation from their leaders. As the leader listens to the employees on sensitive topics, clear, beneficial, and rational communication should be their ultimate goal.

In applying the TEAM LEAD model, the leader must be prepared to step back, listen and let someone else take the lead by delegating his authority and guiding them to explore decisions, ideas, and mistakes. Leaders should let the employees know that a mistake is a learning opportunity; this will help the team take a calculated risk because the leader emphasizes learning from the mistakes. Employees should not be afraid to make mistakes. According to Shaw (2014), great leaders emanate from an ability to make great decisions which comes from making bad decisions and learning from them. An authentic leadership behavior can influence people by creating a culture where everyone can express themselves by sharing mutually beneficial information. Blind spots prevent leaders from being effective.

Image: The Blind Leading the Blind by Pieter Bruegel the Elder, 1568

Leaders must beware of their blind spots by paying attention to their rearview mirror through lessons learned. Leaders must create an environment where the team can identify blind spots through feedback and fix them immediately. Blind spots are personal traits or aspects a leader is unaware of that may limit how they react or behave, limiting their effectiveness. Acknowledging blind spots is always positive. Leaders can turn these weaknesses into strengths with practice—active listening results in effective communication, which is a critical component of the TEAM LEAD model. Leaders must create an environment of open communication to eliminate blind spots that will keep them from effectively leading their teams.

Image: The TEAM LEAD Model Framework

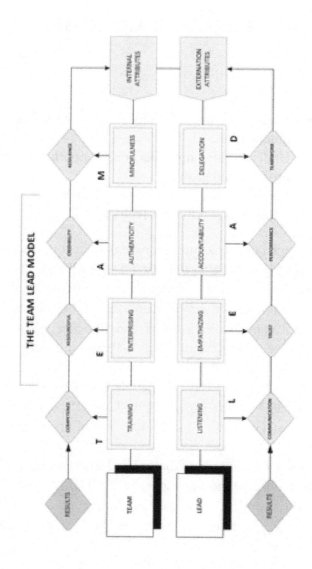

CHAPTER 13

LEADERSHIP REFLECTIONS

Learning Objectives:

- Understand the importance of reflective leadership practices.
- Understanding how this book supports personal and professional growth.
- Identify reflective questions a leader must answer to improve and remain effective.

Reflective practice accelerates improvement in your leadership skills and enables you to better understand yourself and others (Forbes, 2021). Leaders must invest in themselves through self-reflection and take time to intentionally reflect daily and at the end of the year. Leadership reflection makes a leader gain a better understanding of themselves (value principles, knowledge, ability, and skills), learn from past experiences, and adapt and respond to new leadership challenges. In my lifetime I have noticed that people complain a lot about poor leadership or failed leaders. However, we have effective leaders who in their lifetime have made an impact on the life of people either directly or indirectly.

Instead of complaining about failed leadership, I have decided to proffer a solution in the framework of the TEAM LEAD model by embarking on this project years ago. Also, I was curious as to what drives exceptional and successful leaders to be the best. My quest was to discover what tools, approaches, skills, methodologies, or theories prepare those in authority for self-leadership to assist team building and to evaluate those tools, methods, or theories. I wanted this study to contribute to the body of knowledge on the influence of self-leadership and barriers that prevent leaders' team-building abilities. The objective was accomplished by exploring self-leadership influence on team building among leaders in any organization. I was able to examine participants' perceptions of the concept of self-leadership regarding the team-building abilities of leaders in the organization. I have learned a lot during this process, and one thing that stands out is that leadership is about relationships, and how you nurture those relationships is critical.

Personal and professional growth. Conducting this research project has provided individual and professional growth. I hope the readers will find growth as they read this book because this research has a direct and broader impact on business practice in terms of insight into self-leadership as a skill necessary for business success. I can say that this study adds to my personal growth through the knowledge I gained in conducting this research; there is a deeper appreciation of self-leadership and the ability to build a cohesive team. Reflecting on this topic of interest and my self-leadership application, it is important to note that to lead effectively and build a cohesive team, you must be able to relate well with every team member. As I reflect on the role of a leader, I have come to realize that relationships matter in leadership. Aside from relationships, being teachable, enterprising, authentic, and mindful, the ability to actively listen and communicate effectively, be empathetic, accountable for our actions, and the ability to delegate is also critical. What it comes down to is that people want a leader that is trustworthy, credible, and authentic.

For anyone to lead others, they must first have what it takes to lead themselves, and you cannot give what you do not possess. The bottom line is that leadership begins with leading oneself before you are able to influence the lives of others. I remember growing up as a young seminarian, my goal was to be a priest, but I did not understand what it takes to be a priest which is sacrifice and responsibilities. All I knew was the influence the priest around my environment had on so many young people, including myself. Eventually, I got into the minor seminary with the support of my parent and my parish priest. This was where I learned self-leadership, and my ability to lead myself was put to test because the seminary had a daily routine for all the seminarians that required you to lead yourself with a set of guidelines. And of course, it was a boarding school, and they had to come up with activities to keep us busy. One thing I quickly realized was the seminary leadership hierarchy even among the students. We had a Rector and his deputy who were in charge of the affairs of the seminarians. Then there were the senior seminarians who served for a period of one to two years before proceeding to other future assignments. Some minor seminarians had various roles ranging from the senior prefect to storekeeper, prefect in charge of food procurement, the labor prefect, and the chapel prefect. During my time in the minor seminary, I had two positions which were a storekeeper and a prefect in charge of procurement.

Everything I did in my role as a prefect affected my fellow seminarians. For instance, I was responsible for determining the weekly menu for students and the weekly inventory to signal the purchase of additional supplies when the storage room ran out of food. The Rector of the seminary trusted the store prefects and their ability to carry out their functions. There was no way I could have handled these responsibilities and my school work with self-leadership. On the other hand, the seminarians trusted that whenever they get to the dining hall, there will be food available for them to eat. I remember that before becoming a storekeeper, I was once an assistant storekeeper, during which I was mentored by the prefect, which enabled me to build a strong relationship with the former storekeepers and prefects in charge of procurement. It was a matter of time before I became a storekeeper myself. It was not my goal to be a storekeeper, but at the same time, I was not surprised when I got the role, because of the relationship I had built over the years. For me to be in charge of the store, I had to be able to manage myself, my school works, and also the store activities to make sure that the seminarians were fed daily. To be successful in my role as a storekeeper at that young age, I had to be trained by my seniors who were storekeepers before me. I had an enterprising mindset which helped me become resourceful. I was authentic, which helped my credibility because I understood what was required of me as a storekeeper. Also, I was mindful of the environment because being a storekeeper did not excuse me from executing my academic requirement. I was able to listen to what the seminarians preferred to eat and made sure I balanced their diet. I was empathetic to their needs, making sure they didn't starve. I was accountable to the Rector and seminarians. I had to delegate some of the store activities to my assistant, but I made sure I never abandoned my duty as a storekeeper. I shared my seminary experience because as a young adult, I learned that leadership is a privilege that comes with a responsibility portfolio that is supported and maintained with your relationships with others.

> *Leadership is a privilege that comes with a responsibility portfolio that is supported and maintained with the leader's relationships with others.*

These are all the attributes identified in the TEAM LEAD model. I learned a valuable lesson in the seminary that having a strong leadership foundation and effective mentorship is critical. Remember that as a leader, everyone is watching what you do, and you are influencing people either directly or indirectly. When I graduated from the seminary, I served as an auxiliary in the seminary temporarily. This was the waiting period to decide whether to further my studies in the major seminary in pursuit of the priesthood. I remember having a conversation with the Rector and he advised me that no matter what I do in life, I should strive never to be mediocre; and that in any position that needs to be reached, I should aspire to reach that position, and that has always helped in my quest to be an effective leader and excel in any position I find myself. In the words of my late father, Elder Boniface Wolemonwu, "a good name is better than money." My father taught me the importance of integrity and preserving a good name, and the advice of my former Rector guided me in everything I have done to be where I am today. I believe that you can never be an effective leader if you do not have the Team Lead attributes identified in this book, and the research that was conducted proves this fact.

Applying the TEAM LEAD framework to professional practice and implementing positive change is paramount for effective leadership. The lack of self-awareness and the need to understand oneself causes a leader's lack of self-efficacy when addressing a follower's needs (DeWitt, 2018). This book contributes to the body of knowledge on self-leadership influence on team-building abilities among leaders in an organization. In the earlier chapters, we discussed how the TEAM LEAD framework contributes to the body of knowledge relating to the influence of self-leadership in team-building abilities among leaders. The various themes identified support the research questions posed in the earlier chapter. In the analysis, the apparent themes include a preference for developing leadership competency, human skills, self-leadership training, professional skill, self-development, team orientation, and specific learning and growth.

The practical application of what individuals learn effectively improves their talent, especially with low-level prior knowledge of the subject of discussion (Wang & Han, 2021).

> Self-leadership is summarized in 1 Timothy 3:5-6 (NLT) "For if a man cannot manage his own household, how can he take care of God's church? A church leader must not be a new believer, because he might become proud, and the devil would cause him to fail."

In conclusion, there is no leadership without responsibilities, leaders carry a huge burden of responsibility and it can be stressful when things do not go as planned. According to John Maxwell, "everything rises and falls on leadership." Becoming an effective leader takes a lot of work and training. Effective leaders do not buckle under pressure, they excel and have control of themselves with a calming demeanor toward others around them. They respond to a situation calmly and with a well-thought-out plan. They have the capacity to empathize, they are understanding and not afraid to share their feelings with their team members. Every leader must strive to be an effective administrator with a good reputation and be recognized for their humility and fairness.

Every leader should be able to answer some of the following reflective questions to improve and understand why they are in a leadership role:

1. *Why are you serving as a leader?*

   ....

2. *What are you most proud of accomplishing this year, and do you enjoy your leadership role?*

   ....

3. *What is your number one goal as a leader?*

   ....

4. *Who will you recognize in your team and why?*

   ....

The Team Lead Model of Self-Leadership

5. *How do you keep your team motivated and inspired?*

   ....

6. *How will you challenge yourself next year as a leader?*

   ....

7. *What is one decision you regret today as a leader?*

   ....

8. *Why do you do what you do every day as a leader?*

   ....

9. *Who do you look up to for inspiration or mentorship?*

   ....

10. *What qualities do you think you can improve upon as a leader?*

    ....

11. *How are you able to show authenticity, credibility, and trust to the people you are leading?*

    ....

12. *Where did you improve, grow and develop the most in your leadership role?*

....

13. *What do you consider the most crucial attribute that keeps you focused and grounded in your leadership role?*

....

14. *What aspect of your leadership role was unsuccessful, why, and what will you do to fix it?*

....

GLOSSARY

Accountability.

The fact or condition of being accountable. Being responsible for what you do and giving a good reason for it, or the degree to which this happens—an obligation or willingness to accept responsibility for one's actions. The person is taking or being assigned responsibility for something you have done or something you are supposed to do.

Application.

The action of putting something into operation. The application of common sense to a problem. The particular use or purpose to which something is put in practical use or relevance.

Assumption.

To accept something as true or as certain to happen without proof. Something that you assume to be the case, even without proof. For example, people might make the assumption that you're a nerd if you wear glasses, even though that's not true or very nice.

Attributes.

Something is attributed as belonging to a person, thing, and group. This is a quality or feature regarded as a characteristic or inherent part of someone or something. To attribute something to someone/something is to believe that something is the result of a particular situation, event, or person's actions.

Authenticity.

The quality of being authentic, legitimate, trustworthy, or genuine. Worthy of acceptance or belief as conforming to or based on fact. Lack of falsehood or misrepresentation. Of established authority for truth and correctness. When someone is original or real, you're honest with yourself and others without trying to be something you are not fake or trying to be someone else or an imitation.

Barriers.

Anything that prevents or blocks movement from one place to another. A barrier is a fence or other obstacle that prevents movement or access. It can be either natural or artificial, which keeps something from passing through or moving forward.

Benefit.

An advantage or profit gained from something. Anything that produces good or helpful results or effects or that promotes well-being. A benefit is something that will provide an advantage for others, something you may receive as compensation.

Biblical.

Relating to or contained in the Bible. Biblical or Bible-based, scriptural, according to the Scriptures, or the Holy Bible. It resembles the language or style of the Bible. It is in accord with the Bible or when something is in keeping with the nature of the Bible.

Code.

A system of words, letters, figures, or other symbols substituted for other words, letters, etc., especially for the purposes of being discrete. A system of symbols (such as letters or numbers) represents assigned and often secret meanings.

Communication.

The imparting or exchanging of information or news. The act of transferring information from one place, person, or group to another. Every communication involves (at least) one sender, a message, and a recipient. The act or process of using words, sounds, signs, or behaviors to express or exchange information or express your ideas and thoughts.

Competency.

The ability to do something successfully or efficiently. The set of demonstrable characteristics and skills that enable and improve the efficiency or performance of a job. The capability to apply or use the set of related knowledge, skills, and abilities required to perform 'critical work functions or tasks in a defined work setting. Competency means "capability." However, we use it to mean sufficient qualification.

Credibility.

The quality of being trusted and believed. The quality of being believable or worthy of trust. The quality or power of inspiring belief or the capacity for belief and offering reasonable grounds for being believed.

Delegation.

The delegation of authority refers to the division of labor and decision-making responsibility to an individual that reports to a leader. Delegation of authority is the process of transferring responsibility for a task to another employee.

Development.

This is the process of developing or being developed. It is a process that creates growth, progress, positive change, or the addition of physical, economic, environmental, social, and demographic components. To develop is defined as growing or becoming more advanced, or it can mean to cause something to grow.

Embeddedness.

Job embeddedness is the collection of forces that influence employee retention. It can be distinguished from turnover in that its emphasis is on all of the factors that keep an employee on the job, rather than the psychological process one goes through when quitting. E.g., organizations can improve job embeddedness by an enhanced work-life balance policy.

Empathy.

Empathy is the ability to understand and share the feelings of another person. Empathy is the capacity to understand or feel what another person is experiencing from within their frame of reference, that is, the ability to place oneself in another's position.

Enterprising.

The degree of having or showing initiative and resourcefulness. An independent, energetic spirit and a readiness to act, and the drive to recognize opportunities. Good at thinking of and doing new and challenging things, especially things that will benefit someone. An enterprising person sees opportunity in all areas of life. To be enterprising is to keep your eyes open and your mind active.

Growth.

Growth is the process of increasing in physical size. Something that has grown or is growing. A stage or condition in improving, developing, or maturing. A natural method of increasing in size or developing growth. Self-improvement of your skills, knowledge, personal qualities, life goals, and outlook.

Implication.

The conclusion can be drawn from something, although it is not explicitly stated. A possible future effect or result. Something that is suggested without being said directly. Something that is implied. The fact or state of being involved in or connected to something.

Integration.

The act or process of uniting different things. The practice of connecting people from other races in an attempt to give people equal rights and racial integration. An act or instance of combining into an integral whole. Integration refers to the result of a process that aims to stitch together different, often disparate, subsystems.

Leadership.

Leadership is a process of influencing others to achieve a goal. This is the action of leading a group of people or an organization. It is the state or position of being a leader—the process of social influence, which maximizes the efforts of others towards the achievement of a goal.

Limitation.

This is a limiting rule or circumstance, a restriction. A condition of limited ability; a defect or failure. The action of limiting something. An act or instance of limiting. The quality or state of being limited. Something that limits: restraint. A certain period that is limited by the statute.

Mindfulness.

Mindfulness is the quality or state of being conscious or aware of something. Mindfulness practices can help us increase our ability to regulate emotions and decrease stress, anxiety, and depression. It can also help a leader to focus our attention, as well as observe our thoughts and feelings without judgment.

Orientation.

The determination of the relative position of something or someone. The state of being oriented. An introduction to guide one in adjusting to new surroundings, employment, or activity. The ability to locate oneself in one's environment regarding time, place, and people.

Participant.

The person who takes part in something. A participant is someone who takes part in something. An example of a participant is a person participating in an interview in research—a person who takes part in or becomes involved in a particular activity.

Pattern.

A regular and intelligible form or sequence discernible in specific actions or situations. "a complicating factor is the change in working patterns." A pattern is the repeated or regular way in which something happens or is done.

Perception.

The ability to see, hear or become aware of something through the senses. The state of being or the process of becoming aware of something through the senses. A way of regarding, understanding, or interpreting something; a mental impression.

Saturation.

When seeing similar instances repeatedly, the researcher becomes empirically confident that a category is saturated. Saturation means that no additional data are being found whereby the researcher can develop properties of the category. When there is enough information to replicate the study, additional new information has been attained, and further coding is no longer feasible.

Skill.

This ability to do something well; expertise. The ability to use one's knowledge effectively and readily in execution or performance. An ability to do an activity or job well, mainly because you have practiced it. The learned ability to perform an action with determined results with good execution often within a given amount of time, energy, or both.

Teamwork.

Co-operation between those who are working on a task. Teamwork is the collaborative effort to achieve a common goal or complete a job most effectively and efficiently. A team, or a group of interdependent individuals who work together towards a common goal.

Training.

The action of teaching a person or animal a particular skill or type of behavior. Teaching, or developing in oneself or others, any skills and knowledge or fitness related to specific useful competencies. Training has specific goals of improving one's capability, capacity, and productivity.

Trait.

This is a distinguishing quality or physical characteristic, typically one belonging to a person or a genetically determined characteristic. For instance, height, skin color, hair color, and eye color of humans.

Trust.

Trust refers to the firm belief in the reliability, truth, ability, or strength of someone or something. To believe that someone or something is reliable, good, honest, effective, and confident in someone or something. Confidence in the honesty or integrity of a person or thing.

Reflection.

Reflection is a profound thought or consideration—an idea about something, especially one that is written down or expressed. Reflection is a means of processing thoughts and feelings about an incident or a difficult period—an exploration and explanation of events – not just a description.

Resilience.

Resilience is the capacity to recover quickly from difficulties; toughness. The ability to mentally or emotionally cope with a crisis or to return to pre-crisis status quickly.

Resourceful.

To have the ability to find quick and clever ways to overcome difficulties. Resourcefulness is about getting things done in the face of obstacles and constraints. Approaching what's in front of you and optimizing what you have, or whether you're making something new.

REFERENCES

Abreu-Ledon, R., Lujan-Garcia, D., Garrido-Vega, P., & Escobar-Perez, B. (2018). A meta-analytic study of the impact of lean production on business performance. *International Journal of Production Economics*. 200. doi:10.1016/j.ijpe.2018.03.015

Ada, M., & San, B. T. (2018). Comparison of machine-learning techniques for landslide susceptibility mapping using two-level random sampling (2LRS) in alakir catchment area, antalya, turkey. *Natural Hazards*, 90(1), 237-263. doi:10.1007/s11069-017-3043-8

Akverdian, A. (2019). Those humane soft skills: why can't robots replace us? *Talent Acquisition Excellence Essentials*, http://ezproxy.liberty.edu/login?qurl=https%3A%2F%2Fww w.proquest.com%2Fmagazines%2Fthose-humane-soft-skills-why-can-t-robots-replace%2Fdocview%2F2307420676%2Fse-2%3Faccountid%3D12085

Alhassan, I., Sammon, D., & Daly, M. (2018). Data governance activities: A comparison between scientific and practice-oriented literature. *Journal of Enterprise Information Management*, 31(2), 300-316. doi:10.1108/JEIM-01-2017-0007

Alnakhli, H., Singh, R., Agnihotri, R., & Itani, O. S. (2020). From cognition to action: The effect of thought self-leadership strategies and self-monitoring on adaptive selling behavior. *The Journal of Business & Industrial Marketing*, 35(12), 1915-1927. doi:10.1108/JBIM-06-2019-0302

Alves, J.C., Lovelace, K.J., Manz, C.C., Matsypura, D., Toyasaki, F. and Ke, K.(G). (2006), "A cross-cultural perspective of self-leadership", Journal of Managerial Psychology, Vol. 21 No. 4, pp. 338-359. https://doi.org/10.1108/02683940610663123

Ames, H., Glenton, C., & Lewin, S. (2019). Purposive sampling in a qualitative evidence synthesis: A worked example from a synthesis on parental perceptions of vaccination communication. *BMC Medical Research Methodology*, 19(1), 26-9. doi:10.1186/s12874-019-0665-4

Arkolakis, C., Papageorgiou, T., & Timoshenko, O. A. (2018). Firm learning and growth. *Review of Economic Dynamics*, 27, 146-168. doi:10.1016/j.red.2017.06.001

Arli, D., & Sutanto, N. (2018). Investigating the importance of self-acceptance and self-efficacy on weight management in a developing country. *International Journal of Nonprofit and Voluntary Sector Marketing*, 23(2), [e1583]. doi:10.1002/nvsm.1583

Armstrong, J. P., & McCain, K. D. (2021). Narrative pedagogy for leadership education: Stories of leadership efficacy, Self-Identity, and leadership development. *Journal of Leadership Studies (Hoboken, N.J.)*, 14(4), 60-70. doi:10.1002/jls.21724

Assarroudi, A., Heshmati Nabavi, F., Armat, M. R., Ebadi, A., & Vaismoradi, M. (2018). Directed qualitative content analysis: The description and elaboration of its underpinning methods and data analysis process. *Journal of Research in Nursing*, 23(1), 42-55. doi:10.1177/1744987117741667

Asurakkody, T. A., & Kim, S. H. (2020). Effects of knowledge sharing behavior on innovative work behavior among nursing students: Mediating role of self-leadership. *International Journal of Africa Nursing Sciences*, 12, 100190. doi:10.1016/j.ijans.2020.100190

Athanasopoulou, A., Moss-Cowan, A., Smets, M., & Morris, T. (2018). Claiming the corner office: Female CEO careers and implications for leadership development. *Human Resource Management*, 57(2), 617-639. doi:10.1002/hrm.21887

Avey, J. B., Bruce, A. J., & Luthans, F. (2011). Experimentally analyzing the impact of leader positivity on follower positivity and performance. *The Leadership Quarterly*, 22(1), 282-294. doi:10.1016/j.leaqua.2011.02.004.

Bai, Y., Lin, L., & Liu, J. T. (2019). Leveraging the employee voice: A multi-level social learning perspective of ethical leadership. *The International Journal of Human Resource Management*, 30(12), 1869-1901. doi:10.1080/09585192.2017.1308414

Bailey, S. F., Barber, L. K., & Justice, L. M. (2018). Is self-leadership just self-regulation? exploring construct validity with HEXACO and self-regulatory traits: Research and reviews research and reviews. *Current Psychology*, 37(1), 149-161. doi:10.1007/s12144-016-9498-z

Bakker, A. (2019). *Design Research in Education*. London: Routledge, https://doi-org.ezproxy.liberty.edu/10.4324/9780203701010

Banks, J., Wye, L., Hall, N., Rooney, J., Walter, F. M., Hamilton, W., Gjini, A., & Rubin, G. (2017). The researchers' role in knowledge translation: A realist evaluation of the development and implementation of diagnostic pathways for cancer in two united kingdom localities. *Health Research Policy and Systems*, 15(1), 1-11. doi:10.1186/s12961-017-0267-8

Banovic, M., Reinders, M. J., Claret, A., Guerrero, L., & Krystallis, A. (2019). One fish, two fish, red fish, blue fish: How ethical beliefs influence consumer perceptions of blue aquaculture products? *Food Quality and Preference*, 77, 147-158. doi:10.1016/j.foodqual.2019.05.013

Barton, C., Tam, C. W. M., Abbott, P., Hall, S., & Liaw, S. (2017). Can research that is not intended or unlikely to be published be considered ethical? *Australian Family Physician*, 46(6), 442-444.

Beauchamp, M. R., McEwan, D., & Waldhauser, K. J. (2017). Team building: conceptual, methodological, and applied considerations. *Current Opinion in Psychology*, 16, 114-117. doi:10.1016/j.copsyc.2017.02.031

Becker, K. M. (2019). Beyond researcher as instrument: Researcher with instrument: Musicking in qualitative data collection. *Qualitative Research Journal*, 19(4), 426-437. doi:10.1108/QRJ-02-2019-0021

Behjati, S. (2017). First-hands' contribution in business inquiry based on qualitative inquiry of assessing environmentalism initiatives. *Management of Sustainable Development*, 9(1), 39. doi:10.1515/msd-2017-0013

Belayneh, T., Gebeyehu, A., Adefris, M., Rortveit, G., & Genet, T. (2019). Translation, transcultural adaptation, reliability, and validation of the pelvic organ prolapse quality of life (P-QoL) in amharic. *Health and Quality of Life Outcomes*, 17(1), 12-11. doi:10.1186/s12955-019-1079-z

Bendell, B. L., Sullivan, D. M., & Marvel, M. R. (2019). A gender-aware study of self-leadership strategies among high-growth entrepreneurs. *Journal of Small Business Management*, 57(1), 110-130. doi:10.1111/jsbm.12490

Bhardwaj, P. (2019). Types of sampling in research. *Journal of the Practice of Cardiovascular Sciences*, 5(3), 157-163. doi:10.4103/jpcs.jpcs_62_19

Blanchard, K. (2017). Is a lack of self-leadership derailing your organization? *Kenblanchard.com/self-leadership*. Retrieved from https://resources.kenblanchard.com/ebooks/is-a-lack-of-self-leadership-derailing-your-organization

Bracht, E. M., Junker, N. M., & van Dick, R. (2018). Exploring the social context of self-leadership-self-leadership-culture. *Journal of Theoretical Social Psychology*, 2(4), 119-130. doi:10.1002/jts5.33

Bracht, E. M. (2019). I do what is best for us: Can self-leadership-culture impact organizational success? *Academy of Management Proceedings*, (1), 18167. doi:10.5465/AMBPP.2019.18167abstract

Brink, R. (2018). A multiple case design for the investigation of information management processes for work-integrated learning. *International Journal of Work - Integrated Learning*, 19(3), 223.

Retrieved from http://ezproxy.liberty.edu/login?qurl=https%3A%2F%2Fsearch.proquest.com%2Fdocview%2F2227916606%3Facco

Browning, M. (2018). Self-leadership: why it matters. *International Journal of Business and Social Science.* *9(2),* https://ijbssnet.com/journals/Vol_9_No_2_February_2018/2.pdf

Brower, H.H., Schoorman, F.D., and Tan, H.H (2000). A Model of Relational Leadership: The Integration of Trust and Leader–Member Exchange. *The Leadership Quarterly* 11(2):227-250, DOI: 10.1016/S1048-9843(00)00040-0

Bryant, A. (2021). *Self-leadership definition: the practice of intentionally influencing your thinking, feeling, and actions towards your objectives.* Retrieved from https://www.selfleadership.com/what-is-self-leadership#:~:text=self%2dleadership%20definition,leader%20from%20the%20Inside%20Out).

Buchholz, W., & Sandler, T. (2017). Successful leadership in global public good provision: Incorporating behavioral approaches. *Environmental and Resource Economics,* 67(3), 591-607. doi:10.1007/s10640-016-9997-2

Bum, C. (2018). relationships between self-leadership, commitment to exercise, and exercise adherence among sport participants. *Social Behavior and Personality,* 46(12), 1983-1995. doi:10.2224/sbp.7371

Cai, W. J., Loon, M., & Wong, P. H. K. (2018). Leadership, trust in management, and acceptance of change in hong Kong's civil service bureau. *Journal of Organizational Change Management,* 31(5), 1054-1070. doi:10.1108/jocm-10-2016-0215

Campbell, M. (2020). Automated coding: The quest to develop programs that write programs. *Computer,* 53(2), 80-82. doi:10.1109/MC.2019.2957958

Carstensen, A., & Bernhard, J. (2019). Design science research – a powerful tool for improving methods in engineering education research. *European Journal of Engineering Education*, 44(1-2), 85-102. doi:10.1080/03043797.2018.1498459

Cassell, C., Cunliffe, A., & Grandy, G. (2019). Qualitative research in business and management. *SAGE Publications Ltd.* doi.org/10.4135/9781526430236

Cascio, M. A., Lee, E., Vaudrin, N., & Freedman, D. A. (2019). A team-based approach to open coding: Considerations for creating intercoder consensus. *Field Methods*, 31(2), 116-130. doi:10.1177/1525822X19838237

Chabirand, A., Loiseau, M., Renaudin, I., & Poliakoff, F. (2017). Data processing of qualitative results from an interlaboratory comparison for the detection of "flavescence dorée" phytoplasma: How the use of statistics can improve the reliability of the method validation process in plant pathology. *PloS One*, 12(4), e0175247. doi:10.1371/journal.pone.0175247

Chance, P. L. (2009). *Introduction to educational leadership and Organizational, Behavior: Theory into Practice.* (2nd edition). Routledge; New York, NY.

Cheong, A. T., Chinna, K., Khoo, E. M., & Liew, S. M. (2017). Determinants for cardiovascular disease health check questionnaire: A validation study. *PloS One*, 12(11), e0188259. doi:10.1371/journal.pone.0188259

Chernew, M. E., & Landrum, M. B. (2018). Targeted supplemental data collection — addressing the quality-measurement conundrum. *The New England Journal of Medicine*, 378(11), 979-981. doi:10.1056/nejmp1713834

Clark, D. (2015). Stand Out: How to Find Your Breakthrough Idea and Build a Following Around It. *Portfolio.* London, UK.

Collins, J. C. & Porras, J. I. (2004). Built to last: Successful habits of visionary companies.(10th revised edition). *Harper Business.* New York, NY.

Collins, J. C. (2001). Good to Great: Why Some Companies Make the Leap and Others Don't. (1st edition). *Harper Business.* New York, NY.

Coetzer, M. F., Bussin, M., & Geldenhuys, M. (2017). The functions of a servant leader. *Administrative Sciences,* 7(1), 5. doi:10.3390/admsci7010005

Collins, C. S., & Stockton, C. M. (2018). The central role of theory in qualitative research. *International Journal of Qualitative Methods.* doi:10.1177/1609406918797475

Corner, E. J., Murray, E. J., & Brett, S. J. (2019). Qualitative, grounded theory exploration of patients' experience of early mobilization, rehabilitation, and recovery after critical illness. *BMJ Open,* 9(2), e026348. doi:10.1136/bmjopen-2018-026348

Cooper, D., Hamman, J., & Weber, R. (2020). Fool me once: an experiment on credibility and leadership. *The Economic Journal : the Journal of the British Economic Association.* doi:10.1093/ej/ueaa059

Coronado, G., Rivelli, J., Green, B., Petrik, A., Schneider, J., Gokcora, B., & Bigler, K. (2017). System-Level Barriers to Follow-up Colonoscopy Completion After Positive Fecal Test: Interviews With Gastroenterologists and Staff. *Journal of Patient-Centered Research and Reviews.,* 4(3), 157–158. doi:10.17294/2330-0698.1487

Costa, W. F., de Albuquerque Tito, A. L., Brumatti, P.N.M., & Mauro de Oliveira Alexandre, M. L. (2017). The use of data collection instruments in qualitative research: A study of tourism research papers. *Turismo: Visão e Ação,* 20(1), 02-28. doi:10.14210/rtva.v20n1.p02-28

Covelli, B. J., & Mason, I. (2017). Linking theory to practice: authentic leadership. *Academy of Strategic Management Journal,* 16(3), 1-10. Gale Academic OneFile, https://link-gale-com.ezproxy.liberty.edu/apps/doc/A541400289/AONE?u=vic_liberty&sid=AONE&xid=11258189. Accessed 28 June 2020

Crabtree, B. F., Howard, J., Miller, W. L., Cromp, D., Hsu, C., Coleman, K., Austin, B., Flinter M., Tuzzio, L., & Wagner, E. H. (2020). Leading innovative practice: Leadership attributes in LEAP practices. *The Milbank Quarterly*, 98(2), 399-445. doi:10.1111/1468-0009.12456

Cranmer, G. A., Goldman, Z. W., & Houghton, J. D. (2019). I'll do it myself: Self-leadership, proactivity, and socialization. *Leadership & Organization Development Journal*, 40(6), 684-698. doi:10.1108/LODJ-11-2018-0389

Creswell, J.W., and Creswell, J.D. (2017). *Research design: Qualitative, quantitative, and mixed methods approach*. Sage Publications, CA

Cuncic, A. (2020). *How to Develop and Practice Self-Regulation*. https://www.verywellmind.com/how-you-can-practice-self-regulation-4163536

Cunningham, K. B., Kroll, T., & Wells, M. (2018). Development of the cancer-related loneliness assessment tool: Using the findings of qualitative analysis to generate questionnaire items. *European Journal of Cancer Care*, 27(2), e12769-n/a. doi:10.1111/ecc.12769

Cypress, B. (2018). Qualitative research methods: A phenomenological focus. *Dimensions of Critical Care Nursing*. 37(6). doi.10.1097/DCC.0000000000000322

Daud, Y. M. (2020). Self-leadership and its application to today's leader - A review of literature. The Strategic Journal of Business & Change Management, 8 (1), 1 – 11.

Dawson, D., Hepworth, J., Bugaian, L., & Williams, S. (2020). The drivers of higher education leadership competence: A study of moldovan HEI's. *Studies in Higher Education (Dorchester-on-Thames)*, 45(6), 1217-1232. doi:10.1080/03075079.2018.1557135

de Araujo, Diana von Borell, & Franco, M. (2017). Trust-building mechanisms in a coopetition relationship: A case study design. *International Journal of Organizational Analysis*, 25(3), 378-394. doi:10.1108/IJOA-04-2016-1012

Degirmenci, Y. (2018). Examination of main trends in geographical education research in turkey. *Review of International Geographical Education Online*, 8(1), 93-108.

Dempsey, M., & Brafman, O. (2018). Radical Inclusion: What the post-9/11 World Should Have Taught us About Leadership. (1st edition). Missionday. New York, NY.

Denny, E., & Weckesser, A. (2019). Qualitative research: what it is and what it is not. BJOG: *an International Journal of Obstetrics and Gynaecology.*, 126(3), 369–369. doi:10.1111/1471-0528.15198

DePree, M. (2004). Leadership is an art. (Reprint edition). Crown Business Publishing Group. New York, NY.

Dewan, T., & Squintani, F. (2018). Leadership with trustworthy associates. *The American Political Science Review*, 112(4), 844-859. doi:10.1017/S0003055418000229

DeWitt, P. M. (2018). Principals' moral purpose in the context of LGBT inclusion. *Journal of Professional Capital and Community*, 3(1), 2-11. doi:10.1108/JPCC-02-2017-0005

Donahue, P. (2018). *An exploration of the relationship between leader authenticity and trust* (Order No. 13421666). Available from ProQuest Central; ProQuest Central; ProQuest Dissertations & Theses Global. (2154833808). Retrieved from http://ezproxy.liberty.edu/login?url=https://search-proquest-com.ezproxy.liberty.edu/docview/2154833808?accountid=12085

Downer, K., Wells, C., & Crichton, C. (2019). All work and no play: A text analysis. *International Journal of Market Research.* 61(3). doi.10.1177/1470785318821849

Drakeley, A.C. (2018). Follower Commitment: The Impact of Authentic Leadership's Positivity and Justice on Presenteeism. *CORE Scholar*, https://corescholar.libraries.wright.edu/cgi/viewcontent.cgi?article=3333&context=etd_all

Duncan, D., & Klockner, K. (2020). Development of the contributing factors framework interview guide (CFF-IG): All aboard the rail safety truth train. *Safety Science*, 129, 104853. doi:10.1016/j.ssci.2020.104853

Duta, A., & Duta, V. M. (2017). Qualitative methods of research on banking risks. *Finance: Challenges of the Future*, 1(19), 78-87

Dyer, W., & Dyer, J. (2020). *Beyond team building: how to build high performing teams and the culture to support them (First edition.)*. Hoboken, New Jersey: Wiley.

Ebneyamini, S., & Sadeghi Moghadam, M. R. (2018). Toward developing a framework for conducting case study research. *International Journal of Qualitative Methods*, 17(1), 160940691881795. doi:10.1177/1609406918817954

Edirisingha, P. A., Abarashi, J., Ferguson, S., & Aitken, R. (2017). From participant to friend: The role of facebook engagement in ethnographic research. *Qualitative Market Research: An International Journal*, 20(4), 416-434. doi:10.1108/QMR-02-2016-0019

Efthimiou, O. (2017). Heroic ecologies: Embodied heroic leadership and sustainable futures. *Sustainability Accounting, Management, and Policy Journal (Print)*, 8(4), 489-511. doi:10.1108/sampj-08-2015-0074

Eide, A. E., Saether, E. A., & Aspelund, A. (2020). An investigation of leaders' motivation, intellectual leadership, and sustainability strategy in relation to norwegian manufacturers' performance. *Journal of Cleaner Production*, 254, 120053. doi:10.1016/j.jclepro.2020.120053

Elfil, M., & Negida, A. (2017). Sampling methods in clinical research: *an educational review. Emergency*, 5(1), e52-e52. doi:10.22037/emergency.v5i1.15215

Elliott, D., Husbands, S., Hamdy, F. C., Holmberg, L., & Donovan, J. L. (2017). Understanding and improving recruitment to randomized controlled trials: Qualitative research approaches. *European Urology*, 72(5), 789-798. doi:10.1016/j.eururo.2017.04.036

Emde, S. (2020). Production planning for a ramp-up process in a multi-stage production system with worker learning and growth in demand. *International Journal of Production Research*, 1–20. doi:10.1080/00207543.2020.1798034

Engström, K., & Esbensen, K. H. (2018). Evaluation of sampling systems in iron ore concentrating and pelletizing processes – quantification of total sampling error (TSE) vs. process variation. *Minerals Engineering*, 116, 203-208. doi:10.1016/j.mineng.2017.07.008

Engelbrecht, A. S., Heine, G., & Mahembe, B. (2017). Integrity, ethical leadership, trust, and work engagement. *Leadership & Organization Development Journal*, 38(3), 368-379. doi:10.1108/LODJ-11-2015-0237

Escudier, M. P., Woolford, M. J., & Tricio, J. A. (2018). Assessing the application of knowledge in clinical problem-solving: The structured professional reasoning exercise. *European Journal of Dental Education*, 22(2), e269-e277. doi:10.1111/eje.12286

Evans, D. J. R., Pawlina, W., & Lachman, N. (2018). Human skills for human[istic] anatomy: An emphasis on nontraditional discipline-independent skills. *Anatomical Sciences Education*, 11(3), 221-224. doi:10.1002/ase.1799

Feldman, J. A. (2018). An archival review of preferred methods for theory building in follower research. *South African Journal of Economic and Management Sciences*, 21(1), e1-e7. doi:10.4102/sajems.v21i1.1582

Fernandez, A.A., & Shaw, G.P. (2020). Academic leadership in a time of crisis: The coronavirus and covid-19. *Journal of leadership studies, 14(1),* doi:10.1002/jls.21684

Fernandes, F., Carneiro, A., Campos, R. N., Soeiro-de-Souza, M. G., Barros, V. B., & Moreno, R. A. (2019). SIGMA-VB: Validity and reliability of the brazilian portuguese version of the montgomery-åsberg depression rating scale using the structured interview guide for the MADRS. *Revista Brasileira De Psiquiatria*, 41(4), 297-302. doi:10.1590/1516-4446-2018-0105

Ferrari, M., Shakya, Y., Ledwos, C., Kwame, M., & Ahmad, F. (2018). Patients' mental health journeys: A qualitative case study with interactive computer-assisted client assessment survey (iCASS). *Journal of Immigrant and Minority Health*, 20(5), 1173-1181. doi:10.1007/s10903-017-0643-z

Fingleton, N., Duncan, E., Watson, M., & Matheson, C. (2019). Specialist clinicians' management of dependence on non-prescription medicines and barriers to treatment provision: An exploratory mixed methods study using behavioral theory. *Pharmacy*, 7(1), 25. doi:10.3390/pharmacy7010025

Finkelstein, S. (2016). Super bosses: How Exceptional Leaders Master the Flow of Talent. (1st edition). *Portfolio*. London, UK.

FitzPatrick, B. (2019). Validity in qualitative health education research. *Currents in Pharmacy Teaching and Learning*, 11(2), 211-217. doi:10.1016/j.cptl.2018.11.014

Flaming, L., & Mosca, J. (2019). Should accounting majors have human resource training in compliance, coaching, team building and mentoring skills? *Journal of Higher Education Theory and Practice*, 19(5), 73-82. doi:10.33423/jhetp.v19i5.2283

Flores, H. R., Jiang, X., & Manz, C. C. (2018). Intra-team conflict: The moderating effect of emotional self-leadership. *The International Journal of Conflict Management*, 29(3), 424-444. doi:10.1108/IJCMA-07-2017-0065

Forrest, C. K., & Bruner, M. W. (2017). Evaluating social media as a platform for delivering a team-building exercise intervention: A pilot study. *International Journal of Sport and Exercise Psychology*, 15(2), 190-206. doi:10.1080/1612197X.2015.1069879

Foroughi, H., Gabriel, Y., & Fotaki, M. (2019). Leadership in a post-truth era: A new narrative disorder? *Leadership*, 15(2), 135-151. doi:10.1177/1742715019835369

Fortney, C. A., & Steward, D. K. (2017). A qualitative study of nurse observations of symptoms in infants at end-of-life in the neonatal intensive care unit. *Intensive & Critical Care Nursing*, 40, 57-63. doi:10.1016/j.iccn.2016.10.004

Fung, H. P. (2018). The influence of leadership roles and team building & participation on team shared mental models: a study of project managers in Malaysia. *Revista De Administração De Roraima*, 8(2), 230-259. doi:10.18227/2237-8057rarr.v8i2.4736

Furlan Matos Alves, M.W., Lopes de Sousa Jabbour, A.B., Kannan, D. and Chiappetta Jabbour, C. J. (2017). Contingency theory, climate change, and low-carbon operations management. Supply Chain Management: *An International Journal*, 22(3), 223-236. doi:10.1108/SCM-09-2016-0311

Gallagher, S., and Daly, A. (2018). Dynamical Relations in the Self-Pattern. *Front Psychol*. 2018; 9: 664. Published online 2018 May 11. doi: 10.3389/fpsyg.2018.00664

Gallup (2020). *The Relationship Between Engagement at Work and Organizational Outcomes 2020 Q12* Meta-Analysis: Tenth Edition. https://www.gallup.com/workplace/321725/gallup-q12-meta-analysis-report.aspx?thank-you-report-form=1#ite-321731

Ganesh, M. P., M Ángeles, L., & Vázquez-Rodríguez, P. (2019). Are self-leaders more willing to mentor others? A study among Indian and Spanish university teachers. *Cross-Cultural & Strategic Management*, 26(2), 223-245. http://dx.doi.org.ezproxy.liberty.edu/10.1108/CCSM-04-2017-0047

Gannouni, K., & Ramboarison-Lalao, L. (2019). Examining gender effects on leadership among future managers: Comparing hofstede's masculine vs. feminine countries. *Management International*, 23, 42-51. Retrieved from http://ezproxy.liberty.edu/login?qurl=https%3A%2F%2Fsearch.proquest.com%2Fdocview%2F2381636186%3Facco

Gaur, D. (2019). Self-leadership and interpersonal competences of future aspiring professionals in the arab middle east: *Reference to FIRO-B*. *Management Science Letters*, 9(12), 2021-2028. doi:10.5267/j.msl.2019.7.004

Gavin, C.S. (2018). The impact of leadership development using coaching. *Journal of Practical Consulting*, Vol. n Iss. n, pp. 137-147 https://www.regent.edu/acad/global/publications/jpc/vol6iss1/JPC_6-1_Gavin_pgs137-147.pdf

Gao, S., Niu, X., & Li, T. (2017). Analysis of a constant retrial queue with joining strategy and impatient retrial customers. *Mathematical Problems in Engineering*, 2017, 1-8. doi:10.1155/2017/9618215

Gasston-Holmes, B. (2019). The connection between leadership and learning: A middle leader's experience navigating the waters. *Leading and Managing*, 25(1), 15-28, https://search-informit-org.ezproxy.liberty.edu/fullText;dn=757454618968013;res=IELHSS

Gebrihet, T. A., Mesgna, K. H., Gebregiorgis, Y. S., Kahsay, A. B., Weldehaweria, N. B., & Weldu, M. G. (2017). Awareness, treatment, and control of hypertension is low among adults in aksum town, northern ethiopia: A sequential quantitative-qualitative study. *PloS One*, 12(5), e0176904. doi:10.1371/journal.pone.0176904

George, B., & Sims, P. (2007). True North: Discover Your Authentic Leadership. (1st edition). *Jossey-Bass*. San Francisco, CA.

Glaser, J. E. (2014). Conversational Intelligence: How Great Leaders Build Trust and Get Extraordinary Results. *Bibliomotion.* New York, NY

Goisauf, M., Martin, G., Bentzen, H.B., Budin-Ljøsne, I., Ursin, L., Durnová, A., Leitsalu, L., Smith, K., Casati, S., Lavitrano, M., Mascalzoni, D., Boeckhout, M. & Mayrhofer, M.T. (2019). Data in question: A survey of european biobank professionals on ethical, legal, and societal challenges of biobank research, *PloS one*, vol. 14, no. 9, pp. e0221496.

Goldsby, E. A., Goldsby, M. G. & Neck, C. P. (2020). Self-leadership strategies for nurse managers. *Nursing Management,* Springhouse, 51(3), 34–40. doi: 10.1097/01.NUMA.0000654848.10513.11.

Goldsby, E., Goldsby, M., Neck, C. B., & Neck, C. P. (2020). Under Pressure: Time Management, Self-Leadership, and the Nurse Manager. *Administrative Sciences*, 10(3), 38. http://dx.doi.org.ezproxy.liberty.edu/10.3390/admsci10030038

Gordon, J., & Smith, M. (2015). You Win in the Locker Room First: The 7 C's to Build a Winning Team in Business, Sports, and Life. (1st edition). *Wiley Publishing,* New York.

Gray, M. (2017). Applied qualitative research design: A total framework approach roller margaret and lavrakas paul applied qualitative research design: A total framework approach 398pp £36.99 guilford press 9781462515752 1462515754. *Nurse Researcher,* 24(3), 6-6. doi:10.7748/nr.24.3.6.s3

Gray, L. M., Wong-Wylie, G., Rempel, G. R., & Cook, K. (2020). Expanding qualitative research interviewing strategies: Zoom video communications. *The Qualitative Report,* 25(5), 1292-1301. Retrieved from http://ezproxy.liberty.edu/login?qurl=https%3A%2F%2Fwww.proquest.com%2Fdocview%2F2405672296%3Faccountid%3D12085

Grynchenko, M., Ponomaryov, O., & Lobach, O. (2018). leadership as a factor for building a project team. *Innovative Technologies and Scientific Solutions for Industries*, (1 (3)), 13-21. doi:10.30837/2522-9818.2018.3.013

Guenter, H., Gardner, W. L., Davis McCauley, K., Randolph-Seng, B., & Prabhu, V. P. (2017). Shared authentic leadership in research teams: testing a multiple mediation model. *Small-Group Research*, 48(6), 719–765. doi:10.1177/1046496417732403

Guillotin, B., & Mangematin, V. (2018). Authenticity-based strategizing: moving business schools beyond accreditations and rankings. *Journal of Management Development*, 37(6), 480-492. doi:10.1108/JMD-12-2016-0301

Gupta, M., Joshi, A., & Vidya, T. N. C. (2017). Effects of social organization, trap arrangement and density, sampling scale, and population density on bias in population size estimation using some common mark-recapture estimators. *PloS One*, 12(3), e0173609. doi:10.1371/journal.pone.0173609

Gurman, T., Ballard Sara, A., Villanueva Lorenzo, F., Luis, D., Hunter, G., Maloney, S., Fujita-Conrads, R., & Leontsini, E. (2020). The role of gender in zika prevention behaviors in the dominican republic: Findings and programmatic implications from a qualitative study. *PLoS Neglected Tropical Diseases*, 14(3), e0007994. doi:10.1371/journal.pntd.0007994

Gustafsson, J. (2017). Single case studies vs. multiple case studies: a comparative study literature review. *diva-portal.org*. Retrieved from: http://www.diva-portal.org/smash/get/diva2:1064378/FULLTEXT01.pdf

Guznov, S., Lyons, J., Pfahler, M., Heironimus, A., Woolley, M., Friedman, J., & Neimeier, A. (2020). Robot transparency and team orientation effects on human-robot teaming. *International Journal of Human-Computer Interaction*, 36(7), 650-660. doi:10.1080/10447318.2019.1676519

Hao, X., Li, X., & Zheng, J. (2018). Screening china emergency medical team (CEMT) members: A self-leadership perspective. *Prehospital and Disaster Medicine*, 33(6), 596-601. doi:10.1017/S1049023X18000961

Harper, L., & McCunn, R. (2017). Hand in glove: using qualitative methods to connect research and practice. *International Journal of Sports Physiology and Performance.*, 12(7), 990–993. doi:10.1123/ijspp.2017-0081

Harris, D. (2020). *Literature review and research design.* London: Routledge, https://doi-org.ezproxy.liberty.edu/10.4324/9780429285660

Harunavamwe, M., Pillay, D., & Nel, P. (2020). The influence of psychological capital and self-leadership strategies on job embeddedness in the banking industry. *SA Journal of Human Resource Management*, 18, e1-e11. doi:10.4102/sajhrm.v18i0.1294

Hasberry, A. (2019). Self-acceptance in black and white. *Education Sciences*, 9(2), 143. doi:10.3390/educsci9020143

Hashemi-Aliabadi, S., Jalali, A., Rahmati, M., & Salari, N. (2020). Group reminiscence for hope and resilience in care-seekers who have attempted suicide. *Annals of General Psychiatry*, 19, 1-8. doi:10.1186/s12991-020-0257-z

Hastings, E., Jahanbakhsh, F., Karahalios, K., Marinov, D., & Bailey, B. (2018). Structure or nurture?: The effects of team-building activities and team composition on team outcomes. *Proceedings of the ACM on Human-Computer Interaction*, 2(CSCW), 1-21. doi:10.1145/3274337

Hayashi, P., Abib, G., & Hoppen, N. (2019). Validity in Qualitative Research: A Processual Approach. *The Qualitative Report*, 24(1), 98-112. http://ezproxy.liberty.edu/login?qurl=https%3A%2F%2Fww w.proquest.com%2Fdocview%2F2171118565%3Faccountid% 3D12085

Hearn, E. (2019). Leadership credibility and support for u.s. foreign policy: experimental evidence from Japan. *Research & Politics*. doi:10.1177/2053168019858047

Hermansyah, H., Kumaraningrum, A. R., Purba, J. H., Edison, & Yohda, M. (2020). Safety analysis technique for a system with limited data: A case study of the multipurpose research reactor in indonesia. *Energies (Basel)*, 13(8), 1975. doi:10.3390/en13081975

Heizmann, H., & Liu, H. (2018). Becoming green, becoming leaders: Identity narratives in sustainability leadership development. *Management Learning*, 49(1), 40-58. doi:10.1177/1350507617725189

Hilger, A., Rose, M., & Wanner, M. (2018). Changing faces - factors influencing the roles of researchers in real-world laboratories. *Gaia (Heidelberg, Germany)*, 27(1), 138-145. doi:10.14512/gaia.27.1.9

Hoang, T., Liu, J., Pratt, N., Zheng, V. W., Chang, K. C., Roughead, E., & Li, J. (2018). Authenticity and credibility aware detection of adverse drug events from social media. *International Journal of Medical Informatics*, 120, 157-171. doi:10.1016/j.ijmedinf.2018.10.003

Hollander-Rodriguez, J., & DeVoe, J. E. (2018). Family medicine's task in population health: Defining it and owning it. *Family Medicine*, 50(9), 659-661. doi:10.22454/FamMed.2018.868771

Holma, A., Leskinen, P., Myllyviita, T., Manninen, K., Sokka, L., Sinkko, T., & Pasanen, K. (2018). Environmental impacts and risks of the national renewable energy targets – A review and a qualitative case study from finland. *Renewable & Sustainable Energy Reviews*, 82, 1433-1441. doi:10.1016/j.rser.2017.05.146

Horlings, L. G., Nieto-Romero, M., Pisters, S., & Soini, K. (2019). Operationalizing transformative sustainability science through place-based research: The role of researchers. *Sustainability Science*, 15(2), 467-484. doi:10.1007/s11625-019-00757-x

Huang, C., Jia-Chi, H., & Chang, Y. (2019). Team goal orientation composition, team efficacy, and team performance: The separate roles of team leader and members. *Journal of Management and Organization*, 25(6), 825-843. http://dx.doi.org.ezproxy.liberty.edu/10.1017/jmo.2016.62

Huang, L., Tung, H., & Lin, P. (2019). Associations among knowledge, attitudes, and practices toward palliative care consultation service in healthcare staffs: A cross-sectional study. *PloS One*, 14(10), e0223754. doi:10.1371/journal.pone.0223754

Hunt, H., Pollock, A., Campbell, P., Estcourt, L., & Brunton, G. (2018). An introduction to overviews of reviews: Planning a relevant research question and objective for an overview. *Systematic Reviews*, 7(1), 39-9. doi:10.1186/s13643-018-0695-8

Hunt, M. A., Heilman, C. B., Shutran, M., & Wu, J. K. (2017). Commentary: an introduction to leadership self-assessment at the society of neurological surgeons post-graduate year one boot camp: observations and commentary. *Neurosurgery*, 80(3), E201-E204. doi:10.1093/neuros/nyw093

Hunt, J.M., & Weintraub, J.R. (2017). *The coaching manager: developing top talent in business*, SAGE Publications Inc. eBook edition

Hurst, S., Arulogun, O. S., Owolabi, M. O., Akinyemi, R., Uvere, E., Warth, S., & Ovbiagele, B. (2017). Pretesting qualitative data collection procedures to facilitate methodological adherence and team building in nigeria. *International Journal of Qualitative Methods*, 14(1), 53-64. doi:10.1177/160940691501400106

Ibus, S., & Ismail, F. (2018). Conceptual framework: the mediating effect of self-efficacy in the relationships of self-leadership, knowledge sharing, and innovative work behavior. *International Journal of Academic Research in Business and Social Sciences.*, 8(11). doi:10.6007/IJARBSS/v8-i11/5378

Iivari, N. (2018). Using member checking in interpretive research practice: A hermeneutic analysis of informants' interpretation of their organizational realities. *Information Technology & People (West Linn, Or.)*, 31(1), 111-133. doi:10.1108/ITP-07-2016-0168

Ireland, J. D., Deloney, L. A., Renfroe, S., & Jambhekar, K. (2017). The use of team-building activities to build a better resident. *Current Problems in Diagnostic Radiology*, 46(6), 399-401. doi:10.1067/j.cpradiol.2017.02.005

Irwin, T. (2018). Extraordinary Influence: How Great Leaders Bring Out the Best in Others. (1st edition). Hardcover – Wiley. New Jersey.

Jacob, L., & Speed, T. P. (2018). The healthy aging gene expression signature for Alzheimer's disease diagnosis: A random sampling perspective. *Genome Biology*, 19(1), 1-3. doi:10.1186/s13059-018-1481-6

Jamali, H. R. (2018). Does research using qualitative methods (grounded theory, ethnography, and phenomenology) have more impact? *Library & Information Science Research* 40(3–4), 201-207. doi:10.1016/j.lisr.2018.09.002

Janssens, K. A. M., Bos, E. H., Rosmalen, J. G. M., Wichers, M. C., & Riese, H. (2018). A qualitative approach to guide choices for designing a diary study. *BMC Medical Research Methodology*, 18(1), 140-12. doi:10.1186/s12874-018-0579-6

Javed, B., Rawwas, M. Y. A., Khandai, S., Shahid, K., & Hafiz, H. T. (2018). Ethical leadership, trust in leader, and creativity: The mediated mechanism and an interacting effect. *Journal of Management and Organization*, 24(3), 388-405. doi:10.1017/jmo.2017.56

Jentoft, N., & Olsen, T. S. (2019). Against the flow in data collection: How data triangulation combined with a 'slow' interview technique enriches data. *Qualitative Social Work*, 18(2), 179–193. doi:10.1177/1473325017712581

Jennings, K., & Stahl-Wert, J. (2016). The Serving Leader: Five Powerful Actions to Transform Your Team, Business, and Community. (2nd edition). Berrett-Koehler Publishers.

Jones, R. J., Napiersky, U., & Lyubovnikova, J. (2019). Conceptualizing the distinctiveness of team coaching. *Journal of Managerial Psychology*, 34(2), 62-78. doi:10.1108/jmp-07-2018-0326

Jones-Schenk, J. (2018). Relational coordination: beyond teambuilding. *The Journal of Continuing Education in Nursing*, 49(12), 543-544. doi:10.3928/00220124-20181116-03

Johnson, M., Tod, A. M., Brummell, S., & Collins, K. (2018). Discussing potential recurrence after lung cancer surgery: uncertainties and challenges. *European Journal of Cancer Care*, 27(5), e12870-n/a. doi:10.1111/ecc.12870

Joshi, S. (2021). *Self-Leadership*. Retrieved October 2nd, 2021, from https://pt.slideshare.net/p4sl/the-discipline-of-self-leadershipptx/5

Kankanhalli, A. (2020). Artificial intelligence and the role of researchers: Can it replace us? *Drying Technology*, 38(12), 1539-1541. doi:10.1080/07373937.2020.1801562

Karamouz, M., & Olyaei, M. A. (2019). A quantitative and qualitative framework for reliability assessment of waste water treatment plants under coastal flooding. *International Journal of Environmental Research*, 13(1), 21-33. doi:10.1007/s41742-018-0141-8

Karlgaard, R., & Malone, M.S. (2015). Team Genius: The New Science of High-Performing Organizations. *Harper Business Publishing*. New York, NY.

Keats, J. (2019). Leadership and Teamwork. *Obstetrics and Gynecology Clinics*, 46(2), 293–303. doi:10.1016/j.ogc.2019.01.008

Khan, M. R., & Wajidi, A. (2019). Role of leadership and team building in employee motivation at the workplace. *Global Management*

Journal for Academic & Corporate Studies, 9(1), 39-49. Retrieved from http://ezproxy.liberty.edu/login?url=https://search-proquest-com.ezproxy.liberty.edu/docview/2264569963?accountid=12085

Kharasch, E. (2019). Understanding research methods and the readers' toolbox. *Anesthesiology: the Journal of the American Society of Anesthesiologists, Inc.,* 130(2), 181–182. doi:10.1097/ALN.0000000000002588

Kharouf, H., Sekhon, H., Fazal-e-Hasan, S. M., Hickman, E., & Mortimer, G. (2019). The role of effective communication and trustworthiness in determining guests' loyalty. *Journal of Hospitality Marketing & Management,* 28(2), 240-262. doi:10.1080/19368623.2018.1505574

Kim, H., & Kim, K. (2019). Impact of self-efficacy on the self-leadership of nursing preceptors: The mediating effect of job embeddedness. *Journal of Nursing Management,* 27(8), 1756-1763. doi:10.1111/jonm.12870

Klimenko, K., Rosenberg, S. A., Dybdahl, M., Wedebye, E. B., & Nikolov, N. G. (2019). QSAR modelling of a large imbalanced aryl hydrocarbon activation dataset by rational and random sampling and screening of 80,086 REACH pre-registered and/or registered substances. *PloS One,* 14(3), e0213848. doi:10.1371/journal.pone.0213848

Klug, K., Felfe, J., & Krick, A. (2019). Caring for oneself or for others? how consistent and inconsistent profiles of health-oriented leadership are related to follower strain and health. *Frontiers in Psychology,* 10 doi:10.3389/fpsyg.2019.02456

Knight, D. B., & Novoselich, B. J. (2017). Curricular and co-curricular influences on undergraduate engineering student leadership. *Journal of Engineering Education,* 106(1), 44-70. doi:10.1002/jee.20153

Knottnerus, J. A., & Tugwell, P. (2018). Ethics of research methodology requires a methodology of research ethics. *Journal of Clinical Epidemiology*, 100, v-vi. doi:10.1016/j.jclinepi.2018.07.001

Knutson, C. (2020). The foundation of leadership: leading yourself. *The General Leadership*, https://generalleadership.com/foundations-of-leadership/

Koo, H., & Park, C. (2018). Foundation of leadership in asia: Leader characteristics and leadership styles review and research agenda. *Asia Pacific Journal of Management*, 35(3), 697-718. doi:10.1007/s10490-017-9548-6

Komives, S.R., Lucas, N., and McMahon, T.R. (1998). *Exploring leadership: for college students who want to make a difference*. San Francisco: Jossey-Bass Publishers

Kopina, D. (2019). Reinventing organizations: Model of self-organized process organization (SOPO). *Organizacija*, 52(2), 127-141. doi:10.2478/orga-2019-0009

Kör, B. (2016). The mediating effects of self-leadership on perceived entrepreneurial orientation and innovative work behavior in the banking sector. *SpringerPlus*, 5(1), 1-15. doi:10.1186/s40064-016-3556-8

Kotzé, M. (2018). The influence of psychological capital, self-leadership, and mindfulness on work engagement. *South African Journal of Psychology*, 48(2), 279-292. doi:10.1177/0081246317705812

Kunißen, K. (2019). From dependent to independent variable: A critical assessment of operationalizations of 'Welfare stateness' as macro-level indicators in multilevel analyses. *Social Indicators Research*, 142(2), 597-616. doi:10.1007/s11205-018-1930-3

Land, S. K. (2019). The importance of deliberate team building: A project-focused competence-based approach. *IEEE Engineering Management Review*, 47(2), 18-22. doi:10.1109/EMR.2019.2915600

Lane, S. (2018). A good study starts with a clearly defined question. *BJOG: an International Journal of Obstetrics and Gynecology.*, 125(9), 1057–1057. doi:10.1111/1471-0528.15196

Larsson, J., & Björk, S. (2017). Swedish fathers choosing part-time work. *Community, Work & Family.*, epub ahead of print (2). 20(2), 142–161. https://www-tandfonline-com.ezproxy.liberty.edu/doi/full/10.1080/13668803.2015.1089839

Leavens, E. L. S., Stevens, E. M., Brett, E. I., Molina, N., Leffingwell, T. R., & Wagener, T. L. (2019). Use of rideshare services to increase participant recruitment and retention in research: Participant perspectives. *Journal of Medical Internet Research*, 21(4), e11166. doi:10.2196/11166

Lee, M. K., Park, S. Y., & Choi, G. (2020). Association of self-leadership and planning with performing an exercise in patients with colorectal cancer: a cross-sectional study. *Cancer Nursing*, 43(1), E1-E9. doi:10.1097/NCC.0000000000000673

Lee, Y., & Paunova, M. (2017). How learning goal orientation fosters leadership recognition in self-managed teams: A Two-Stage mediation model. *Applied Psychology*, 66(4), 553-576. doi:10.1111/apps.12101

Lesinger, F. Y., Altinay, F., Altinay, Z., Dagli, G. (2018). Examining the role of leadership, trust for school culture, and policy. *Quality & Quantity*, 52(S2), 983-1006. doi:10.1007/s11135-017-0553-0

Lin, C. (2017). A multi-level test for social regulatory focus and team member creativity: Mediating role of self-leadership strategies. *Leadership & Organization Development Journal*, 38(8), 1057-1077. doi:10.1108/LODJ-05-2016-0125

Ling, Q., Liu, F., & Wu, X. (2017). Servant versus authentic leadership: assessing effectiveness in china's hospitality industry. *Cornell Hospitality Quarterly*, 58(1), 53-68. doi:10.1177/1938965516641515

Little, C. (2020). Undergraduate research as a student engagement springboard: Exploring the longer-term reported benefits of participation in a research conference. *Educational Research*, 62(2), 229-245. doi:10.1080/00131881.2020.1747360

Lock, I., & Seele, P. (2018). Gauging the rigor of qualitative case studies in comparative lobbying research. A framework and guideline for research and analysis. *Journal of Public Affairs*, 18(4), e1832-n/a. doi:10.1002/pa.1832

Lovett, S., & Robertson, J. (2017). Coaching using a leadership self-assessment tool. *Leading & Managing*, 23(1), 42-53

Lynch, C. (2019). *Ecclesial leadership as friendship (1st ed.)*. New York: Routledge. doi:10.4324/9780429019357

Maggio, L. A., Artino, A. R., Watling, C. J., Driessen, E. W., & O'Brien, B. C. (2019). Exploring researchers' perspectives on authorship decision making. *Medical Education*, 53(12), 1253-1262. doi:10.1111/medu.13950

Magpili-Smith, N. (2017). Diversity team building: impact on virtual team performance (Order No. 10623764). Available from ProQuest Central; *ProQuest Central; ProQuest Dissertations & Theses Global*. (2018401903). Retrieved from http://ezproxy.liberty.edu/login?url=https://search-proquest-com.ezproxy.liberty.edu/docview/2018401903?accountid=12085

Maher, C., Hadfield, M., Hutchings, M., & de Eyto, A. (2018). Ensuring rigor in qualitative data analysis: A design research approach to coding combining NVivo with traditional material methods. *International Journal of Qualitative Methods*, 17(1), 160940691878636. doi:10.1177/1609406918786362

Mainous, A.G. (2018). Let's reconceptualize how leadership training fits with teamwork and cooperation. *Fam Med.* 2018;50(4):257-258. doi:10.22454/FamMed.2018.265534.

Malik, M., & Azmat, S. (2019). Leader and leadership: historical development of the terms and critical review of literature. 5. 16-32.

Malheiro, B., Guedes, P., Silva, M. F., & Ferreira, P. (2019). Fostering professional competencies in engineering undergraduates with EPS@ISEP. *Education Sciences*, 9(2), 119. doi:10.3390/educsci9020119

Manino, E., Tran-Thanh, L., & Jennings, N. R. (2019). On the efficiency of data collection for multiple naïve bayes classifiers. *Artificial Intelligence*, 275, 356-378. doi:10.1016/j.artint.2019.06.010

Marvel, M. R., & Patel, P. C. (2018). Self-leadership and overcoming the time resource constraint: Accelerating innovation for new products. *IEEE Transactions on Engineering Management*, 65(4), 545-556. doi:10.1109/TEM.2017.2690818

Marques, J. (2017). Toward intuitive self-leadership: Monitoring actions through values and reflection. *Organization Development Journal*, 35(3), 15-41. Retrieved from http://ezproxy.liberty.edu/login?qurl=https%3A%2F%2Fsearch.proquest.com%2Fdocview%2F2002996564%3Faccountid%3D12085

Marx, S. (2017). *Qualitative research in STEM*. New York: Routledge, https://doi-org.ezproxy.liberty.edu/10.4324/9781315676449

Matsumura, T., & Ogawa, A. (2017). Inefficient but robust public leadership. *Journal of Industry, Competition and Trade*, 17(4), 387-398. doi:10.1007/s10842-017-0248-1

Maximo, N., Stander, M. W., & Coxen, L. (2019). Authentic leadership and work engagement: the indirect effects of psychological safety and trust in supervisors. *South African Journal of Industrial Psychology*, 45(1). Retrieved from https://link-gale-com.ezproxy.liberty.edu/apps/doc/A591360458/AONE?u=vic_liberty&sid=AONE&xid=9a413b11

Mayor, E., Daehne, M., & Bianchi, R. (2019). How perceived substance characteristics affect ethical judgment toward cognitive enhancement. *PloS One*, 14(3), e0213619. doi:10.1371/journal.pone.0213619

McChrystal, S., Collins, T., Silverman, D., & Fussell, C. (2015). Team of Teams: New Rules of Engagement for a Complex World. (1st edition). Portfolio Publishing. London, UK.

McEvoy, D. (2018). *Populations and samples: A guide to business statistics.* Hoboken, NJ: John Wiley & Sons, Inc. doi:10.1002/9781119447054.ch2

McEwan, D., Ruissen, G. R., Eys, M. A., Zumbo, B. D., & Beauchamp, M. R. (2017). The effectiveness of teamwork training on teamwork behaviors and team performance: a systematic review and meta-analysis of controlled interventions. *PLoS One*, 12(1) doi:10.1371/journal.pone.0169604

McKim, C. A. (2017). The value of mixed methods research: A mixed methods study. *Journal of Mixed Methods Research*, 11(2), 202-222. doi:10.1177/1558689815607096

Menon, R., Mourougavelou, V., & Menon, A. (2018). Improving medical students' participation in research. *Advances in Medical Education and Practice*, 9, 65-67. doi:10.2147/AMEP.S158758

Miller, C. J., Kim, B., Silverman, A., & Bauer, M. S. (2018). A systematic review of team-building interventions in non-acute healthcare settings. *BMC Health Services Research*, 18(1), 146-21. doi:10.1186/s12913-018-2961-9

Misra, S., & Srivastava, K. B. L. (2018). Team-building competencies, personal effectiveness and job satisfaction: The mediating effect of transformational leadership and technology. *Management and Labour Studies*, 43(1-2), 109-122. doi:10.1177/0258042X17753178

Mitilian, E., Malli, F., & Verger, P. (2020). Image of the new vaccination obligation through the media. *Vaccine*, 38(3), 498-511. doi:10.1016/j.vaccine.2019.10.069

Montgomery, E.T., Mensch, B., Musara, P., Hartmann, M., Woeber, K., Etima, J., & van der Straten, A. (2017). Misreporting of product adherence in the MTN-003/VOICE trial for HIV prevention in africa: Participants' explanations for dishonesty. *AIDS and Behavior*, 21(2), 481-491. doi:10.1007/s10461-016-1609-1

Moreno-Gómez, J., & Calleja-Blanco, J. (2018). The relationship between women's presence in corporate positions and firm performance: The case of colombia. *International Journal of Gender and Entrepreneurship*, 10(1), 83-100. doi:10.1108/IJGE-10-2017-0071

Mortensen, K., & Hughes, T. L. (2018). Comparing Amazon's mechanical turk platform to conventional data collection methods in the health and medical research literature. *Journal of General Internal Medicine:* JGIM, 33(4), 533-538. doi:10.1007/s11606-017-4246-0

Mouton, N. (2019). A literary perspective on the limits of leadership: Tolstoy's critique of the great man theory. *Leadership*, 15(1), 81-102. doi:10.1177/1742715017738823

Mulder, L. (2019). Personal and situational variables of leadership development. *Lablogatory*, Retrieved from https://labmedicineblog.com/2019/01/20/personal-and-situational-variables-of-leadership-development/

Müller, T., & Niessen, C. (2019). Self-leadership in the context of part-time teleworking. *Journal of Organizational Behavior,* 40(8), 883-898. doi:10.1002/job.2371

Mwita, K., Mwakasangula, E., & Tefurukwa, O. (2018). The Influence of Leadership on Employee Retention in Tanzania Commercial Banks. *International Journal of Human Resource Studies.*, 8(2). doi:10.5296/ijhrs.v8i2.12922

Nadelson, S., & Nadelson, L. (2019). Making qualitative research real to students: Using social media postings to teach qualitative data coding. *Worldviews on Evidence-Based Nursing*, 16(2), 169-171. doi:10.1111/wvn.12356

Na-Nan, K., & Saribut, S. (2020). Validation of employees' self-leadership using exploratory and confirmatory factor analysis. *The International Journal of Quality & Reliability Management*, 37(4), 552-574. doi:10.1108/IJQRM-10-2018-0287

Neck, C. P., Manz, C. C., & Houghton, J. D. (2017). *Self-leadership: the definitive guide to personal excellence,* Los Angeles; London: SAGE Publications.

Nederveen Pieterse, A., Hollenbeck, J. R., van Knippenberg, D., Spitzmüller, M., Dimotakis, N., Karam, E. P., & Sleesman, D. J. (2019). Hierarchical leadership versus self-management in teams: Goal orientation diversity as a moderator of their relative effectiveness. *The Leadership Quarterly*, 30(6), 101343. doi:10.1016/j.leaqua.2019.101343

Nghe, M., Hart, J., Ferry, S., Hutchins, L., & Lebet, R. (2020). Developing leadership competencies in midlevel nurse leaders: An innovative approach. *The Journal of Nursing Administration*, 50(9), 481-488. doi:10.1097/NNA.0000000000000920

Nidhi, Sisodia, B. V. S., Singh, S., & Singh, S. K. (2017). Calibration approach estimation of the mean in stratified sampling and stratified double sampling. *Communications in Statistics - Theory and Methods*, 46(10), 4932-4942. doi:10.1080/03610926.2015.1091083

Niedbalski, J. (2017). From a qualitative researcher's workshop—the characteristics of applying computer software in studies based on the grounded theory methodology. *Przegląd Socjologii Jakościowej*, XVIII(2), 46-61.

Noe, M. H., & Gelfand, J. M. (2018). Research techniques made simple: Pharmacoepidemiology research methods in dermatology.

Journal of Investigative Dermatology, 138(2), e13-e18. doi:10.1016/j.jid.2017.10.026

Northouse, P.G. (2019). *Leadership: theory and practice.* Eighth Edition. SAGE Publication, inc.

Öhman, A., Keisu, B., & Enberg, B. (2017). Team social cohesion, professionalism, and patient-centeredness: Gendered care work, with special reference to elderly care - a mixed-methods study. *BMC Health Services Research*, 17(1), 381-12. doi:10.1186/s12913-017-2326-9

Omanovic, V. (2019). The emergence and evolution of researcher identities: Experiences, encounters, learning, and dialectics. *Qualitative Research in Organizations and Management.* 14(2). doi.10.1108/QROM-09-2017-1566

Pak, K., Desimone, L. M., & Parsons, A. (2020). An integrative approach to professional development to support college- and career-readiness standards. *Education Policy Analysis Archives*, 28, 111. doi:10.14507/epaa.28.4970

Palacios, J., Lee, G., Duaso, M., Clifton, A., Norman, I., Richards, D., & Barley, E. (2017). Internet-Delivered Self-management Support for Improving Coronary Heart Disease and Self-management–Related Outcomes. *Journal of Cardiovascular Nursing.*, 32(4), E9–E23. doi:10.1097/JCN.0000000000000392

Pang, J., & Ring, H. (2020). Automated coding of implicit motives: A machine-learning approach. *Motivation and Emotion.*, 44(4), 549–566. doi:10.1007/s11031-020-09832-8

Parker, E. (2017). Finding your inner 'line leader'. *Arkansas Business*, 34(37), 19. Retrieved from https://link-gale-com.ezproxy.liberty.edu/apps/doc/A507966239/ITOF?u=vic_liberty&sid=ITOF&xid=87b65784

Partridge, D. (2015). People Over Profit: Break the System, Live with Purpose, Be More Successful. Thomas Nelson Publishing. Nashville, TN.

Parvin, A. (2019). Leadership and management in quality assurance: Insights from the context of khulna university, bangladesh. *Higher Education,* 77(4), 739-756. doi:10.1007/s10734-018-0299-1

Pattamadilok, C., Planton, S., & Bonnard, M. (2019). Spoken language coding neurons in the visual word form area: Evidence from a TMS adaptation paradigm. *NeuroImage (Orlando, Fla.),* 186, 278-285. doi:10.1016/j.neuroimage.2018.11.014

Pavlovic, Z.M. (2019). Self-leadership: behave like a leader until you become one. *Heruka.* Retrieved on July 2020 from https://herukahealthinnovations.com/2019/05/07/self-leadership-behave-like-a-leader-until-you-become-one

Peragine, J., & Hudgins, G. (2017). 365 no or low-cost workplace team-building activities: Games and exercises designed to build trust and encourage teamwork among employees (Revised Second edition.). *Atlantic Publishing Group, Inc.*

Petty, J. (2017). Emotion work in qualitative research: Interviewing parents about neonatal care. *Nurse Researcher,* 25(3), 26-30. doi:10.7748/nr.2017.e1532

Phillips, T., Saunders, R. K., Cossman, J., & Heitman, E. (2019). Assessing trustworthiness in research: A pilot study on CV verification. *Journal of Empirical Research on Human Research Ethics,* 14(4), 353-364. doi:10.1177/1556264619857843

Pina e Cunha, M., Pacheco, M., Castanheira, F., & Rego, A. (2017). Reflexive work and the duality of self-leadership. *Leadership (London, England),* 13(4), 472-495. doi:10.1177/1742715015606511

Pollastri, A., & Maffenini, W. (2018). Estimation of the percentage of aid received from the food bank using a stratified sampling. *Social Indicators Research,* 136(1), 41-49. doi:10.1007/s11205-016-1514-z

Popov, S. (2019). When is unconditional self-acceptance a better predictor of mental health than self-esteem? *Journal of Rational-*

Emotive & Cognitive-Behavior Therapy, 37(3), 251-261. doi:10.1007/s10942-018-0310-x

Prendergast, M., Welsh, W. N., Stein, L., Lehman, W., Melnick, G., Warda, U., Shafer, M., Ulaszek, W., Rodis, E., Abdel-Salam, S., & Duvall, J. (2017). Influence of organizational characteristics on success in implementing process improvement goals in correctional treatment settings. *The Journal of Behavioral Health Services & Research*, 44(4), 625-646. doi:10.1007/s11414-016-9531-x

Pretorius, S., Steyn, H., & Bond-Barnard, T. J. (2017). Exploring project-related factors that influence leadership styles and their effect on project performance: A conceptual framework. *South African Journal of Industrial Engineering*, 28(4), 95-108. doi:10.7166/28-4-1778

Prominski, M., & Seggern, H. v. (2019). *Design research for urban landscapes: theories and methods.* Abingdon, Oxon; New York, NY; Routledge.

Pylväs, L., & Nokelainen, P. (2021). Academics' perceptions of intercultural competence and professional development after international mobility. *International Journal of Intercultural Relations*, 80, 336-348. doi:10.1016/j.ijintrel.2020.10.004

Qian, J., Li, X., Wang, B., Song, B., Zhang, W., Chen, M., & Qu, Y. (2018). A role theory perspective on how and when goal-focused leadership influences employee voice behavior. *Frontiers in Psychology*, 9, 1244. doi:10.3389/fpsyg.2018.01244

Quinn, R. E. (2004). Building the Bridge as You Walk on It: A Guide for Leading Change. (1st edition). Jossey-Bass. San Francisco, CA.

Rahman, W.A.W.A. (2016). Empathy and Trust: Into a Better Workplace Environment, Journal of Business and Economics, ISSN 2155-7950, USA, December 2016, Volume 7, No. 12, pp. 2025-2034, DOI: 10.15341/jbe (2155-7950)/12.07.2016/009

Ramamoorthi, B., Jäppinen, AK. & Taajamo, M. (2021). Co-sensing and co-shaping as shared and relational practices in bringing about relational leaders in higher education. SN Soc Sci 1, 211 https://doi.org/10.1007/s43545-021-00210-w

Rambe, P., Modise, D. L., & Chipunza, C. (2018). The combined influence of self-leadership and locus of control on the job performance of the engineering workforce in a power generation utility: An empirical perspective. *SA Journal of Human Resource Management*, 16(2), e1-e9. doi:10.4102/sajhrm.v16i0.952

Rapaport, B. (2017). Three Historical Leaders Whose Accountability Equaled Personal Responsibility. Real-time Perspectives. https://www.linkedin.com/pulse/three-historical-leaders-whose-accountability-equaled-rapaport/

Rasdi, R. M., Hamzah, S. R., & Yean, T. F. (2020). Exploring self-leadership development of malaysian women entrepreneurs. *Advances in Developing Human Resources*, 22(2), 189-200. doi:10.1177/1523422320907048

Ratan, S., Anand, T., & Ratan, J. (2019). Formulation of research question - stepwise approach. *Journal of Indian Association of Pediatric Surgeons*, 24(1), 15-20. doi:10.4103/jiaps.JIAPS_76_18

Ready, D. A. (2019). Why Great Leaders Focus On Mastering Relationships: Great leaders are distinguished by their ability to master personal relationships. *MIT Sloan Management Review*. https://sloanreview.mit.edu/article/why-great-leaders-focus-on-mastering-relationships/

Reed, B. N., Klutts, A. M., & Mattingly, T. J., 2nd (2019). A Systematic Review of Leadership Definitions, Competencies, and Assessment Methods in Pharmacy Education. American journal of pharmaceutical education, 83(9), 7520. https://doi.org/10.5688/ajpe7520

Roberts, R. E. (2020). Qualitative interview questions: Guidance for novice researchers. *Qualitative Report*, 25(9), 3185-3203.

Roberts, K., Dowell, A., & Nie, J. (2019). Attempting rigor and replicability in thematic analysis of qualitative research data; a case study of codebook development. *BMC Medical Research Methodology*, 19(1), 66-8. doi:10.1186/s12874-019-0707-y

Roberts, R. M., Fawcett, L., & Searle, A. (2019). An evaluation of the effectiveness of the personal leadership program designed to promote positive outcomes for adolescents. *Journal of Happiness Studies*, 20(3), 743-757. doi:10.1007/s10902-018-9971-5

Rodrigues, A. B., Cunha, G. H. d., Aquino, Caroline Batista de Queiroz, Rocha, S. R., Mendes, C. R. S., Firmeza, M. A., & Grangeiro, Alex Sandro de Moura. (2018). Head and neck cancer: Validation of a data collection instrument. *Revista Brasileira De Enfermagem*, 71(4), 1899-1906. doi:10.1590/0034-7167-2017-0227

Rogers, R. H. (2018). Coding and writing analytic memos on qualitative data: A review of johnny saldaña's the coding manual for qualitative researchers. *The Qualitative Report*, 23(4), 889-892. Retrieved from http://ezproxy.liberty.edu/login?qurl=https%3A%2F%2Fww w.proquest.com%2Fdocview%2F2036388128%3Faccountid% 3D12085

Roll, A. E., & Bowers, B. J. (2017). Promoting healthy aging of individuals with developmental disabilities: A qualitative case study. *Western Journal of Nursing Research*, 39(2), 234-251. doi:10.1177/0193945916668329

Rose, J., & Johnson, C. W. (2020). Contextualizing reliability and validity in qualitative research: Toward more rigorous and trustworthy qualitative social science in leisure research. *Journal of Leisure Research*, 51(4), 432-451. doi:10.1080/00222216.2020.1722042

Rosser, E., Grey, R., Neal, D., Reeve, J., Smith, C., & Valentine, J. (2017). Supporting clinical leadership through action: The nurse consultant role. *Journal of Clinical Nursing*, 26(23-24), 4768-4776. doi:10.1111/jocn.13830

Roysircar, G., Thompson, A., & Boudreau, M. (2017). Born black and male: Counseling leaders' self-discovery of strengths. *Counselling Psychology Quarterly*, 30(4), 343-372. doi:10.1080/09515070.2016.1172204

Rüzgar, N. (2019). leadership traits of Suleiman the magnificent, in terms of great man theory. *Journal of Ottoman Legacy Studies*, 6(15) http://dx.doi.org/10.17822/omad.2019.128

Saffran, L., Hu, S., Hinnant, A., Scherer, L. D., & Nagel, S. C. (2020). Constructing and influencing perceived authenticity in science communication: Experimenting with a narrative. *PloS One*, 15(1), e0226711. doi:10.1371/journal.pone.0226711

Salas, E., Reyes, D., & McDaniel, S. (2018). The science of teamwork: progress, reflections, and the road ahead. *American Psychologist.*, 73(4), 593–600. doi:10.1037/amp0000334

Sanyal, S., & Hisam, M.W. (2018). The impact of teamwork on work performance of employees: A study of faculty members at Dhofar University. *Journal of Business and Management, 20(3), Ver. I, 15-22, doi: 10.9790/487X-2003011522*

Sawin, K. J., Weiss, M. E., Johnson, N., Gralton, K., Malin, S., Klingbeil, C., & Schiffman, R. F. (2017). Development of a Self‑Management Theory-Guided discharge intervention for parents of hospitalized children. *Journal of Nursing Scholarship*, 49(2), 202-213. doi:10.1111/jnu.12284

Saxena, R. (2017). Muddling through the passage of qualitative research: Experiences of a novice researcher. *Vision*. 21(3). doi.10.1177/0972262917721423

Scheithauer, M., Muething, C. S., Silva, M. R., Gerencser, K. R., Krantz, J., & Call, N. A. (2019). Using caregiver report on the impact of challenging behavior exhibited by children with autism spectrum disorder to guide treatment development and outcomes. *International Journal of Developmental Disabilities*, 65(4), 265-276. doi:10.1080/20473869.2018.1428521

Schildcrout, J., Schisterman, E., Mercaldo, N., Rathouz, P., & Heagerty, P. (2018). Extending the case-control design to longitudinal Data. *Epidemiology.*, 29(1), 67–75. doi:10.1097/EDE.0000000000000764

Schmidt, B., Herr, R. M., Jarczok, M. N., Baumert, J., Lukaschek, K., Emeny, R. T., Ladwig, K. (2018). Lack of supportive leadership behavior predicts suboptimal self-rated health independent of job strain after ten years of follow-up: Findings from the population-based MONICA/KORA study. *International Archives of Occupational and Environmental Health*, 91(5), 623-631. doi:10.1007/s00420-018-1312-9

Schmidt, E. (2018). Breadwinning as care? the meaning of paid work in mothers' and fathers' constructions of parenting. *Community, Work & Family,* 21(4), 445-462. doi:10.1080/13668803.2017.1318112

Shrestha, U., Weber, T. L., & Hanson, J. D. (2018). But problems dwell so the urge is constant qualitative data analysis of the OST CHOICES program. *Alcoholism, Clinical and Experimental Research*, 42(9), 1807-1814. doi:10.1111/acer.13837

Schoonenboom, J., & Johnson, R. B. (2017). How to construct a Mixed methods research design. *Kölner Zeitschrift Für Soziologie Und Sozialpsychologie*, 69, 107-131. doi:10.1007/s11577-017-0454-1

Sechelski, A. N., & Onwuegbuzie, A. J. (2019). A call for enhancing saturation at the qualitative data analysis stage via the use of multiple qualitative data analysis approaches. *Qualitative Report*, 24(4), 795-821

Sesen, H., Tabak, A., & Arli, O. (2017). Consequences of self-leadership: A study on primary school teachers. *Kuram Ve Uygulamada Egitim Bilimleri*, 17(3), 945-968. doi:10.12738/estp.2017.3.0520

Shaw, R.B. (2014). *Leadership Blindspots: How Successful Leaders Identify and Overcome the Weaknesses That Matter*, Publishers: Jossey-Bass. 9781118646298

Shirbagi, N. (2018). An assessment of the skill needs of a sample of iranian school principals based on a successful leaders' self-development model. *Pedagogika* (Vilnius, Lithuania), 130(2), 76-91. doi:10.15823/p.2018.23

Sigrid, E., & Weibler Jürgen. (2020). Understanding (non)leadership phenomena in collaborative inter-organizational networks and advancing shared leadership theory: An interpretive grounded theory study. *Business Research,* 13(1), 275-309. doi:10.1007/s40685-019-0086-6

Singh, A.P. (2009). Personality Traits as Predictor of Leadership Effectiveness among Information Technology Professionals. *Indian Journal of Social Science Researches,* Vol. 6, No. 2, Oct., 2009, pp. 57-62, ISSN: 0974-9837.

Smith, A., Purna, J. R., Castaldo, M. P., Ibarra-Rios, D., Giesinger, R. E., Rios, D. R., Weisz, D. E., Jain, A., El-Khuffash, A.F., McNamara, P. J. (2019). Accuracy and reliability of qualitative echocardiography assessment of right ventricular size and function in neonates. *Echocardiography (Mount Kisco, N.Y.),* 36(7), 1346-1352. doi:10.1111/echo.14409

Smith, S. (2018). Is it possible for managers to coach effectively in a hostile culture? *International Journal of Evidence-Based Coaching and Mentoring* Special Issue 12, doi:10.24384/000539

Song, D., Im, J., Lee, J., & Kwon, H. (2018). The impact of entrepreneurial spirit on the willingness to start up via utilizing knowledge and information by college students: Focused on self-leadership mediating effect and regulating effect of gender. *International Journal of Knowledge Content Development & Technology*, 8(4), 33-53. doi:10.5865/IJKCT.2018.8.4.033

Sowey, E. & Petocz, P. (2017). A panorama of statistics: Perspectives, puzzles, and paradoxes in statistics. Place of publication not identified: *John Wiley and Sons, Inc.* Retrieved from https://onlinelibrary-wiley-com.ezproxy.liberty.edu/doi/book/10.1002/ 9781119335139

Spiers, J., Morse, J. M., Olson, K., Mayan, M., & Barrett, M. (2018). Reflection/Commentary on a past article: "Verification strategies for establishing reliability and validity in qualitative research": Http://journals.sagepub.com/doi/full/10.1177/160940690200 100202. *International Journal of Qualitative Methods*, 17(1), 160940691878823. doi:10.1177/1609406918788237

Steckler, E., & Clark, C. (2019). Authenticity and corporate governance. *Journal of Business Ethics*, 155(4), 951-963. doi:10.1007/s10551-018-3903-5

Stedman, M. (2019). The limitations of inclusive research in practice: Reappraising the sympathetic researcher role in applied theatre research. Research in Drama Education: *The Journal of Applied Theatre and Performance*, 24(4), 465-471. doi:10.1080/13569783.2019.1653177

Stelling-Konczak, A., Vlakveld, W. P., van Gent, P., Commandeur, J. J. F., van Wee, B., & Hagenzieker, M. (2018). A study in real traffic examining glance behavior of teenage cyclists when listening to music: Results and ethical considerations. Transportation Research. Part F, *Traffic Psychology and Behaviour*, 55, 47-57. doi:10.1016/j.trf.2018.02.031

Stewart, G.L., Courtright, S.H., & Manz, C.C. (2019). Self-leadership: a paradoxical core of organizational behavior. *Annual Review of Organizational Psychology and Organizational Behavior*, 6:47-67, doi:10.1146/annurev-orgpsych-012218-015130

Stoffelen, A. (2019). Disentangling the tourism sector's fragmentation: A hands-on coding/post-coding guide for interview and policy document analysis in tourism. *Current Issues in Tourism*, 22(18), 2197-2210. doi:10.1080/13683500.2018.1441268

Stowell, S. J., and Mead, S. S. (2020), What People Want in a Leader: How Do You Measure Up? Modern Leaders. https://trainingindustry.com/magazine/mar-apr-2020/what-people-want-in-a-leader-how-do-you-measure-up/#:~:text=Our%20research%20reinforces%20the%20long, people%20want%20leaders%20with%20integrity.&text=Over%2030%25%20of%20respondents%20indicated,accountability%20%E2%80%94%20are%20important%20leadership%20characteristics

Strickland, W., Takerei, S., Pirret, A., Christophers, E., Duplan, K., Avatea, R., Boyd. S., & Greaves, R. (2017). Patients' and families' perception of a need for a patient and/or family initiated rapid response service: A case study design. *Australian Critical Care*, 30(2), 130-131. doi:10.1016/j.aucc.2017.02.059

Stuckey, H. (2018). The second step in data analysis: Coding qualitative research data. *Journal of Social Health and Diabetes*, 3(1), 007-010. doi:10.4103/2321-0656.140875

Taber, K. S. (2018). Lost and found in translation: Guidelines for reporting research data in an 'other' language. *Chemistry Education Research and Practice*, 19(3), 646-652. doi:10.1039/c8rp90006j

The 60-second marketer: 6 reasons why team building is an important part of every business (2017). *Chatham: Newstex*. Retrieved from http://ezproxy.liberty.edu/login?url=https://search-proquest-com.ezproxy.liberty.edu/docview/1949735128?accountid=12085

Theofanidis, D., & Fountouki, A. (2018). Limitations and delimitations in the research process. *Perioperative Nursing*, (GORNA), E-ISSN:2241-3634, 7(3),155–162. http://doi.org/10.5281/zenodo.2552022

Thomas, J. d., Lal, A., Mishra, A. K., Thapa, S. S., & Mosser, G. (2019). Teamwork in medicine. *The New England Journal of Medicine*, 380(23), 2280-2282. doi:10.1056/NEJMc1904676

Thompson, R. A. (2009). Doing What Doesn't Come Naturally: The Development of Self-Regulation. Zero to Three (J), v30 n2 p33-39 Nov 2009. https://eric.ed.gov/?id=EJ915174

Tran, V., Porcher, R., Tran, V., & Ravaud, P. (2017). Predicting data saturation in qualitative surveys with mathematical models from ecological research. *Journal of Clinical Epidemiology*, 82, 71-78.e2. doi:10.1016/j.jclinepi.2016.10.001

Trichas, S., Schyns, B., Lord, R., & Hall, R. (2017). "Facing" leaders: Facial expression and leadership perception. *The Leadership Quarterly*, 28(2), 317-333. doi:10.1016/j.leaqua.2016.10.013

Tross, S., Pinho, V., Lima, J. E., Ghiroli, M., Elkington, K. S., Strauss, D. H., & Wainberg, M. L. (2018). Participation in HIV behavioral research: Unanticipated benefits and burdens. *AIDS and Behavior*, 22(7), 2258-2266. doi:10.1007/s10461-018-2114-5

Turunen, P., & Hiltunen, E. (2019). Empowering leadership in a university spin-off project: A case study of team building. *South Asian Journal of Business and Management* Cases, 8(3), 335-349. doi:10.1177/2277977919876734

Uhl-Bien, M. (2006). Relational Leadership Theory: Exploring the social processes of leadership and organizing. *The Leadership Quarterly* 17:6, pp. 654-676: doi 10.1016/j.leaqua.2006.10.007

UKEssays. (2018). *Theories of self-leadership*. Retrieved from https://www.ukessays.com/essays/business/self-assessment-in-self-leadership-business-essay.php?vref=1

Ureña, C., & Georgiev, I. (2018). Stratified sampling of projected spherical caps. *Computer Graphics Forum*, 37(4), 13-20. doi:10.1111/cgf.13471

Uzman, E., & Maya, İ. (2019). Self-leadership strategies as the predictor of self-esteem and life satisfaction in university students. *International Journal of Progressive Education*, 15(2), 78-90. doi:10.29329/ijpe.2019.189.6

Van Hala, S., Cochella, S., Jaggi, R., Frost, C. J., Kiraly, B., Pohl, S., & Gren, L. (2018). Development and validation of the foundational healthcare leadership self-assessment. *Family Medicine*, 50(4), 262-268. doi:10.22454/FamMed.2018.835145

Vass, C., Rigby, D., & Payne, K. (2017). *The role of qualitative research methods in discrete choice experiments: a systematic review and survey of authors.* Los Angeles, CA: *SAGE* Publications. doi:10.1177/0272989X16683934

Vidal, G. G., Campdesuñer, R. P., Rodríguez, A. S., & Vivar, R. M. (2017). Contingency theory to study leadership styles of small businesses owner-managers at santo domingo, ecuador. *International Journal of Engineering Business Management*, 9, 184797901774317. doi:10.1177/1847979017743172

Vogl, S., Zartler, U., Schmidt, E., & Rieder, I. (2018). Developing an analytical framework for multiple-perspective, qualitative longitudinal interviews (MPQLI). *International Journal of Social Research Methodology*, 21(2), 177-190. doi:10.1080/13645579.2017.1345149

Waldner, D., Cyr, J., Koivu, K., & Goertz, G. (2019). Review symposium: Multimethod research, causal mechanisms, and case studies. *European Political Science*, 18(1), 157-169. doi:10.1057/s41304-017-0147-2

Wang, D., & Han, H. (2021). Applying learning analytics dashboards based on process-oriented feedback to improve students' learning effectiveness. *Journal of Computer Assisted Learning*, 37(2), 487-499. doi:10.1111/jcal.12502

White, M. C., Randall, K., Avara, E., Mullis, J., Parker, G., & Shrime, M. G. (2018). Clinical outcome, social impact, and patient expectation: A purposive sampling pilot evaluation of patients in benin seven years after surgery. *World Journal of Surgery*, 42(5), 1254-1261. doi:10.1007/s00268-017-4296-9

Williams, J. B. W., & Kobak, K. A. (2018). Development and reliability of a structured interview guide for the montgomery-åsberg depression rating scale (SIGMA). *British Journal of Psychiatry*, 192(1), 52-58. doi:10.1192/bjp.bp.106.032532

Williams, J. S., & Lowman, R. L. (2018). The efficacy of executive coaching: An empirical investigation of two approaches using the random assignment and a switching-replications design. *Consulting Psychology Journal: Practice and Research,* 70(3), 227–249. doi:10.1037/cpb0000115

Wolgemuth, J. R., Hicks, T., & Agosto, V. (2017). Unpacking assumptions in research synthesis: A critical construct synthesis approach. *Educational Researcher,* 46(3), 131-139. doi:10.3102/0013189X17703946

Worrall, D. (2013). *Accountability Leadership: How Great Leaders Build a High-Performance Culture of Accountability and Responsibility* (The Accountability Code Series). Kindle Edition.

Woodgate, R. L., Zurba, M., & Tennent, P. (2017). Worth a thousand words? advantages, challenges, and opportunities in working with photovoice as a qualitative research method with youth and their families. *Forum, Qualitative Social Research,* 18(1)

Wu, S., & Bakos, A. (2017). The native hawaiian and pacific islander national health interview survey: Data collection in small populations. *Public Health Reports* (1974), 132(6), 606-608. doi:10.1177/0033354917729181

Wyatt, M., & Silvester, J. (2018). Do voters get it right? A test of the ascription-actuality trait theory of leadership with political elites. *The Leadership Quarterly,* 29(5), 609-621. doi:10.1016/j.leaqua.2018.02.001

Xu, J., & Montague, E. (2019). An experimental study on individual and group affect in multi-tasking teams. *Ergonomics,* 62(3), 376-390. doi:10.1080/00140139.2018.1544378

Zhang, X. C., Lee, H., Rodriguez, C., Rudner, J., Chan, T. M., & Dimitrios, P. (2018). Trapped as a group, escape as a team: applying gamification to incorporate team-building skills through an 'escape room' experience. *Cureus,* doi:10.7759/cureus.2256

Zheng, B., Liu, X., Sun, Y. F., Su, J., Zhao, Y., Xie, Z., & Yu, G. (2017). Development and validation of the chinese version of dry eye related quality of life scale. *Health and Quality of Life Outcomes*, 15(1), 145-7. doi:10.1186/s12955-017-0718-5

Zhou, Q., Mao, J., & Tang, F. (2020). Don't be afraid to fail because you can learn from it! how intrinsic motivation leads to enhanced self-development and benevolent leadership as a boundary condition. *Frontiers in Psychology*, 11, 699. doi:10.3389/fpsyg.2020.00699

Zhu, J., Hu, D., Yin, Y., Zhu, Z., Wang, N., & Wang, B. (2019). HIV prevalence and correlated factors among male clients of female sex workers in a border region of china. *PloS One*, 14(11), e0225072. doi:10.1371/journal.pone.0225072

Zhu, C., Ishikami, S., Zhao, H., & Li, H. (2019). Multichannel long-period fiber grating realized by using the helical sampling approach. *Journal of Lightwave Technology*, 37(9), 2008-2013. doi:10.1109/jlt.2019.2897314

Zigarmi, D. (2018). *The Importance of self-leadership and how to leverage it to improve organizational leadership*. Retrieved from https://medium.com/@dzigarmi/the-importance-of-self-leadership-and-how-to-leverage-it-to-improve-organizational-leadership-f32ffb64938c

ABOUT THE AUTHOR

Dr. Joe Wolemonwu is a career federal employee with the U.S. Department of Defense and the author of "Leveraging Knowledge Management for Effective Customer Service." He is the chairperson of the non-profit, Association of Certified Knowledge Management Professionals (ACKMP). He was a featured speaker at the 2020 Smart Customer Service Conference in Washington, Dc. He has participated as a speaker in multiple Youth Summits and Tech Expos. Also featured as the key speaker at U.S. Department of Defense and U.S. Department of Veterans Affairs conferences. He served in various leadership capacities in the Toastmasters International club, U.S.A. Dr. Wolemonwu is a proponent of the adaptive and relational leadership approach. He is actively involved in his local community and church, where he is involved in the Sunday School and facilitating leaders' training and mentorship for young adults. The foundation of his leadership and professional career started with ExxonMobil Corporation, USA, where he trained and mentored several managers before transitioning into Civil Service to work for the D.C. Government Office of the State Superintendent of Education, the U.S. Marine Corps, and the U.S. Treasury Department. Dr. Wolemonwu is a trained Senior Business Analyst and has worked in several consulting roles. Dr. Wolemonwu obtained his Doctor of Business Administration (DBA) degree from the Liberty University. He holds a Master of Business Administration (MBA) degree from Strayer University and a Bachelor of Science degree in accounting. He is a Certified Knowledge Manager (CKM) and Certified Knowledge Management Professional (CKMP). He has a professional certificate in Strategic Management from the College of Williams and Mary, Williamsburg, VA, and a certificate in Multi-Criteria Decision-Making (MCDM) from the Naval Postgraduate School (NPS) Monterrey, CA.

INDEX

Accountability 13,18-21
Andrew Carnegie 14
Avey Bruce & Luthans 4
Authenticity 9,18-20,40,74-75
Awareness 10
Acceptance 10
Assumption 41
Asurakkody & Kim 60
Arli & Sutano 63
Athanasopoulou, Moss-cowan, Smets & Morris 63-66
Backlander, Rosengren & Kaulio 58
Bailey, Barber & Justice 56, 57
Bakkar 35
Barack Obama 12
Basilica 12
Beanchamp, McEwan & Waldhauser 39
Beatrice Web 12
Behavioral Theory 47
Behavior Focused Strategy 52
Bendell, Sullivan & Marvel 26,53-55
Benevolence 66
Bill Gate 7
Blanchard 28
Bracht, Junker & van Dick 59
Brink 34
Brower, Schoorman & Tan 49
Browning 25-27,43-49,76
Bryant 27, 51
Buchholz & Sandler 47
Bum 68-69
CareerKey 8
Cashman's Theory 46
Charles C. Manz 50
Chatham-Newstex 28
Clark 17
Cold War 13
Foroughi, Gabriel & Fotaki 53
Forest & Bruner 69-70
Foundation 26
Frederick Douglas 10

Conceptual Framework 6
Constructive Thought Strategy 68
Contingency Theory 48
Communication 11
Collins & Stockton 29, 32
Cooper, Hamman & Weber 37-38, 74
Coronavirus 11
Covelli & Mason 40
Crabtree, Howard, Miller, Cromp, Hsu, Coleman, Austin, Flinter, Tuzzio & Wagner 28
Credibility 9, 18, 37-40
Cresswell & Cresswell 30-34
Dave Lewis 11
David Ogilvy 14
Delegation 14, 18-21
Delimitation 42
Dewan & Squintani 58
Dewitt 28
Donald Rumsfeld 14
Donahue 37
Drakeley 74
Dyer & Dyer 28
Eide, Saether & Aspelund 45
Eleanor Roosevelt 13
Engelbrecht, Heine & Mahembe 40
Enterprising 8, 18-19
Empathy 12, 18-21
Employee Viewpoint 3
Ethical Value 10
External construct 11
Facebook 11
Feldman 53
Fernandez & Shaw 40
Fingleton, Duncan, Watson & Matheson 47
Finklestein 16-17
Forbes Magazine 10
Jooste & Frantz 46-59
Job Satisfaction 60
Jones-Schenk 28
Joshua, 24

Fung 27, 70
Furlan, Matos Alves, Lopes De Sousa Jabbour, Kannan & Chiappetta Jabbour 48
Gannouni & Ramboarison-lalao 50
Gasston-Holmes 62-63
George W. Bush 14
Gerald Ford 14
Giovanni Bernadone 12
Glaser 16
Goetzer, Bussin & Geldenhuys 40
Goldsby, Goldsby, Neck, 30-51
Gordon & Smith 16 – 17
Great Man Theory 45
Grimeley, Cochrane, Keane, Sumner, Mullan & O'Connell 71
Gustafsson 31-35
Harris 35
Harry Truman 13
Harper & McCunn 31
Hasberry 63
Hastings, Jahanbakhsh, Karahalios, Marinov & Bailey 71
Hearn 37
Hiroshima 13
Hoang, Lui, Pratt, Zheng, Chang, Ronghead, Li 39
Hunt, Heilman, Shutan & Wu, 26, 61
Hunt & Weintraub 44
Ibus & Ismail 39
Internal Construct, 6
Intrinsic Motivation, 57
ISO 9001:2018, 7
Ireland, Deloney, Renfroe & Jambhekar, 70-71
Irwin 16-17
Jacinda Ardern 11
Jamali 29-30
Jennings & Stahl-wert 17
John F. Kennedy, 7
Johnson, Tod, Brummell & Collins 35-36
Mayiams, Raffo, Clark, 24-40
McChrystal, Collins, Silverman & Fussell, 17
McEwan, Ruissen, Eys, Zumbo & Beauchamp, 38
Mentorship, 14
Mindfulness, 10, 18-20
Montgomery, Mensch, Musara, Hartmann, Woeber, Etima, & Van der Straten, 41

Jones, Napiersky & Lyubovnikova, 69-76
Karlgaard & Malone, 17
Keats, 71
Khan & Wajidi, 27
Kharouf, Sekhon, Fazal-e-Hasan, Hickman & Mortimer, 71
Knight & Novoselich, 28
Knottnerus & Tugwell, 36
Knutson, 26
Koo & Park, 53
Komives, Lucas, McMahon, 49
Kotze, 49
Kim & Kim, 60
Klug, Felfe & Krick, 60-61
Lacroix & Armin, 53
Land 23
Lane, 36
Larsson & Bjork, 33
Leadership, 16-17
Leader-Follower Relationship, 4
Learning Organization, 7
Lee & Paunova, 23
Lee, Park, & Choi, 53-54
Lesinger, Attinay, Altinay & Dagali, 41
Leslie, 17
Ling, Liu, Wu, 40
Limitation, 41
Listening, 11, 20
Lovette & Robertson, 62
Lynch, 23-24
Mahatma Gandhi, 9
Magpili-Smith, 38, 78
Malheiro, Guedes, Silva & Ferreira, 72
Martin Luther King Jr., 9
Marx, 29
Marques, 50
Marvel & Patel, 57
Matsumura & Ogawa, 28-29
Maximo, Stander & Coxen, 36
Rosser, Grey, Neal, Reeve, Smith & Valantine, 15-26
Roysircar, Thompson & Boudreau, 61-62
Ruzgar, 45-46
Sanyal & Hisam, 75
Satyagraha, 9
Schmidt, Herr, Jarczok, Baumert, Lukaschek, Emeny & Ladwig, 28

Moreno-Gomez & Calleja-Blanco, 48-49
Mouton, 45
MPQLI, 33
Mulder, 73
Muller & Niessen, 36
Nagasaki, 13
Natural reward strategy, 68
Neck, Manz & Houghton, 50
Nelson Mandela, 9-10
New Zealand, 11
Nwita, Nwakasangula, Tafurukwa, 77
Ohman, Keisu, Enberg, 31
Palacios, Lee, Duaso, Clifton, Norman, Richard & Barley, 64
Parker, 37-40, 74
Parvin, 29
Patridge, 16-17
Pavlovic, 67-68
Peragine & Hudgin, 38, 75
Personal Leadership, 55-56
Peter Drucker, 11
Peter M. Serge, 7
Pilgrimage, 12
Popov, 64
Prominski & Seggern, 35
Qian, Li, Wang, Song, Zhang, Chen & Qu, 49
Rahman, 12
Rambe, Modise, & Chipunze, 15, 73-77
Rasdi, Hamzah & Yean, 49-51
Relational Theory, 49
Resourceful, 8-18
RSLQ, 51
Richard Branson, 11-15
Vidal, Campdesuñer, Rodriguez & Vivar, 48
Van Hala, Cochella, Jaggi, Frost, Kiraly, Gren & Pohl, 61
Virgin Group, 11
Vogl, Zartler, Schmidt & Riedir, 33
Vroom-Yetton-Jago, 48
Wagner, 28
Walt Disney, 8
Williams & Lowman, 43
Winston Churchill, 10
Wolgemuth, Hick & Agosto, 41
Worrall, 13
World War Two, 10
Woodgate, Zurba, Tennent, 34

Swain, Weiss, Johnson, Gralton, Malvin, Klingbeil & Schiffman, 65
Self-acceptance, 15, 63
Self-assessment, 61
Self-care, 60, 1
Self-confidence, 9
Self-development, 64-66, 94
Self-discovery, 61
Self-efficacy, 60
Self-focused, 58
Self-growth, 15
Self-leadership, 15, 36, 57, 60-73
Self-leadership measure, 52
Self-management, 15, 57, 64
Self-reflection, 56
Self-influence, 57
Shirbagi, 65
Sigrid & Weibler Jurgen, 44-45
Singh, Singh & Banergi, 68
Smith, 65
St. Peter Basilica, 12
Stewart, Courtright & Manz, 26-27
Super-bosses, 16
Team Building Activities, 29, 39, 70
Team building Intervention, 15, 69
Team Characteristics, 64
Tanveer Naseer, 12
Teamwork, 14, 18, 38, 71-75
Theofanidis & Fountouki, 41-42
Thomas, Lal, Mishra, Thapa & Mosser, 71
Trait theory, 46
Trichas, Schyns, Lord & Hall, 47
Trust, 12, 21, 38-40
Uhl-Bien, 49
Uzman, & Maya, 59-67, 94
Ukessays, 61

List of Figures
Conceptual Framework, Figure 1 – Page 6
Team Lead Model Process Flow, Figure 2 – Page 19, 122
Relationship to construct, Figure 3 – Page 39
The benefit of LDP, Figure 4 – Page 88
Self-leadership benefits, Figure 5 – Page 89
Self-leadership influence, Figure 6 – Page 93
How self-leadership enhances growth, Figure 7 – Page 94

Wood Personnel Service, 14
Wyatt & Silvester, 46-47
YSCOUTS, 9
Yu & Ko, 72-73
Zaech & Baldegger, 74, 93
Zhang, Lee, Rodriguez, Rudner, Chan, & Dimitrios, 70
Zhou, Mao & Tang, 65-66

Barriers to self-leadership, Figure 8 – Page 97
How to overcome leadership barrier, Figure 9 - Page 98
Benefits of Leadership Training, Figure 10 – Page 101
Participants' opinion on self-leadership Training, Figure 11 –
Page 103

List of Tables

Theoretical Team Lead Attributes, Table 1 - Page 5
Participants' demographics, Table 2 – Page 84
Participants Training, Table 3 – Page 84
Participants' training benefits, Table 4 – Page 85
Participants' other training, Table 5 – Page 85
How training was conducted, Table 6 – Page 86
Training Curriculum, Table 6 – Page 86
Identified Leadership Style, Table 7 – Page 91
Participants' response on overcoming self-leadership barriers, Table 9 – Page 99

AT A GLANCE

Chapter 1 // The TEAM LEAD Model – Page 1

This chapter identifies the eight-core attributes of the TEAM LEAD Model. The framework of the TEAM LEAD model focuses on a leader getting good **training** to be *competent*, having an **enterprising** mindset to be *resourceful*, being **authentic** to have *credibility*, adopting **mindful** practices to be more *resilient*; actively **listening** to *communicate* effectively, being **empathetic** to gain *trust*, be **accountable** and hold people responsible for improving *performance* and **delegate** authority to promote *teamwork*.

Chapter 2 // Significance of TEAM LEAD Model – Page 24

This chapter will help you learn how to improve your emotional intelligence and be a better leader. You will learn to identify several traits that are incredibly helpful for leaders to possess and become better leaders. You will learn how a leader can attract, inspire, and ultimately retain as much talent as possible. You will learn how to build a cohesive team by applying the framework of the TEAM LEAD Model.

Chapter 3 // Core Leadership Theory – Page 45

This chapter discusses core leadership theories and scholarly literature on leadership. Explored the following leadership theories: The great man theory, trait theory, behavioral theory, contingency theory, influence theory, and relational theory. Leadership theories seek to explain how and why certain people become leaders. Such theories often focus on the characteristics of leaders, and some identify the behaviors that people can adopt to improve their leadership abilities.

Chapter 4 // Origin of Self-leadership – Page 52

This chapter discusses the origin of self-leadership by exploring and reviewing several academic works of literature in the past and present. The chapter began by sharing Charles C Manz's definition of self-leadership. Charles Manz was the first to use the term 'Self-leadership' in 1983 and defined it as; "a comprehensive self-influence perspective that concerns leading oneself." A person has self-leadership skills when he has foresight and makes the right decisions and choices to achieve his goals.

Chapter 5 // Self-leadership Perception – Page 61

This chapter explores how various authors and leaders view the concept of self-leadership. Self-leadership shows a full mediating effect on the relationships between participating in knowledge-sharing activities, and human resources; academics fundamentally refers to driven motivation. It also addresses the core pillars of self-leadership, such as self-

The Team Lead Model of Self-Leadership

determination, self-discovery, self-awareness, self-assessment, self-development, and self-management.

Chapter 6 // Self-Leadership Strategy – Page 69

This chapter explores various frameworks that examine the self-leadership strategies that leaders need to be effective. The chapter discussed the following: Behavior-focused strategies. Constructive thought strategies. Natural reward strategies. It also explored Team Building Intervention. Team-building activities. Teamwork. Communication. Self-leadership constructs. Concludes the chapter with an analysis of Academic Literature on self-leadership strategies.

Chapter 7 // Analysis of Findings – Page 83

This chapter discussed the research finding and explored various themes identified during the data collection and analysis: Leadership competence. Human Skill. Self-leadership. Professional skill. Leadership training can help leaders in making the right decision. Defines self-development as the training obtained from adapting to various leadership styles. Team orientation is being able to navigate daily crises as a team. Concluded with Learning and Growth.

Chapter 8 // Self-leadership Pattern – Page 111

This chapter explores the self-leadership pattern discovered during the research. Self-leadership pattern as developed in the TEAM LEAD model holds that self-care is a relational leadership trait that people develop due to the desire to achieve personal goals in life consciously. A person can predict leadership effectiveness. The findings revealed that openness to experience emerged as the best predictor of leadership effectiveness.

Chapter 9 // Leadership is about Relationships – Page 116

This chapter explores the traits of a relational leader that encourages their team members to accomplish the goal if they make up their minds. The leader must use team engagement, bonding time, and team-building activities to encourage the team by pointing out progress and celebrating the team's successes. The traditional leadership theories emphasize the what and how, while relational leadership focuses on the who. TEAM LEAD model through relational leadership to address the leadership gap.

Chapter 10 // Leadership blind spots – Page 120

This chapter explores leadership blind spots. Defines leadership blind spots as the specific areas where a leader lacks or misses something—concluded that every leader has blind spots. The fact is that even a great leader could have blind spots. A blind spot can be a lack of attention to a specific area or a part of the leader's skill set that never really developed for them to be competent. Leaders must encourage open communication to eliminate blind spots that will keep them from effectively leading their teams.

Chapter 11 // Application of Self-leadership – Page 126

This chapter explores how to apply the self-leadership concept that has risen to prominence in recent years due to the increased awareness of its importance for leaders in making more responsible decisions. It addressed the inclusion of self-leadership training in the Leadership Development Program curriculum of any organization. The research question discussed further the benefit of a leadership development program and self-leadership training.

Chapter 12 // Reflection on Leadership – Page 135

This last chapter explores some questions that reflect some fundamental leadership characteristics. Integrating faith into the business function examined in this study means holding myself to a high ethical and moral behavior standard. Finally, there was a discussion on how to acquire those core self-leadership attributes to be successful. In summary, this book emphasizes applying the TEAM LEAD framework to professional practice and its implications for change.

Made in the USA
Middletown, DE
17 April 2024